I0824614

What I Made for Dinner

ALSO BY KRYS MALCOLM BELC

The Natural Mother of the Child

What I Made for Dinner

A memoir

Krys Malcolm Belc

Catapult · New York

What I Made for Dinner

This is a work of nonfiction. However, correspondence has been shortened for clarity, and dialogue has been reconstructed from memory.

Grateful acknowledgment is made to the following publications for publishing earlier versions of the following chapters: "Sara" as "On Sara Moulton" in *beestung magazine*; "Ree" as "On the Pioneer Woman" in *Electric Literature*; excerpts of "Deb" as "I Made Marcella Hazan's Bolognese" and "I Made Chicken Soup" in *The Kenyon Review*.

First Catapult edition: 2026

ISBN: 978-1-64622-341-1

Library of Congress Control Number: 2026931368

Jacket design by Farjana Yasmin
Jacket images: ingredients © Getty Images / Fatima Guisado lozano; basil © iStock / artisteer
Book design by tracy danes

Catapult
New York, NY
books.catapult.co

Printed in the United States of America

10 9 8 7 6 5 4 3 2 1

for Anna Joan Belc,
my pandemic sourdough

Contents

Stella

It began simply, as my daily mandate: I was home with the kids, three of them, and so now was on the hook for feeding five people, but especially the children, those too young to purchase and prepare their own meals, every single day of my life. Some days it was a joy, sitting down to a perfect breakfast or lunch or dinner, each individual finding what they needed out of these moments around the table. Other times, I was flustered or angry or sad, flailing around the kitchen, nearly throwing a grilled cheese across the table at a child, while Anna prepped to run out the door for another night shift, irritated that in the midst of all that was wrong with the world, there could never be an evening I was not on the hook for yet another meal. Mostly, though, being asked for dinner, for dessert, being called to wake up ready to crack some eggs into a pan, was a neutral element of my existence, like brushing my teeth, like sliding my feet into my shoes before I left the house.

There had been love before, for food and for handing someone you love a bowl of stew or a chocolate chip cookie at the exact moment they needed it. It began when I made my very first dinner for my parents and my siblings—I was twelve—and accelerated and slowed throughout my young adult life. There was learning to carve my mother's Thanksgiving turkey, slice her Christmas roast. There were the months in college when I learned to make ravioli and could think of little else. That pliant yellow dough, making the pasta look beautiful. There was the thrill, in my first year living in an apartment, of whipping mayonnaise by hand, of realizing condiments were something you could *make*, in a bowl, by the power of your own muscle.

But in early 2020, I found myself working at a new job, thinking of so many other things that some days my mandate to make dinner barely registered. I was in a lively shared office at a pediatric oncology clinic, just removed from the patient care areas. I would meet with families during their visits with psychologists or medical providers, and I would give them school advice, would coordinate the flow of information from their medical teams to their schools. In a large clinic staffed mostly by brilliant scientific thinkers, I was the one K–12 teacher. I came to work in my teacher clothes: slim khakis, oxfords, colorful ties, Vans sneakers. I walked the clinic with purpose.

Between patients, when the volume was slow in those first few months, I printed and read research articles at my desk. I learned about the ways oncological treatments impact children's functioning in school, both during and after treatment. The effects of chemotherapy and radiation, I learned, persist for years, and I memorized the names of chemotherapy agents and cancer subtypes included in the most prescient research. I stared at these new words: *intrathecal*, *sequelae*. Slowly I began to recognize the names of parts of the human brain, things to which I had never dedicated any of my thoughts. Two of my favorite words: *supratentorial*, the parts of the brain above the tentorium cerebelli; and *infratentorial*, the parts below. In the years after college, I was a special education teacher and had worked in four schools, all of them chaotic and exhausting, intermittently wonderful in their own ways. In the clinic, my job was not to work as fast as possible, running from class to class, from reading group to reading group, but rather to apply expertise with precision and care. I now had rows of medically oriented browser tabs, articles stapled and neatly filed in manila folders, to help me learn about oncology topics—the names of the chemotherapy agents and regimens responsible for the biggest long-term educational deficits, the ways psychologists and educators had begun to mitigate these treatment sequelae—and special education laws in the states neighboring my own, where I had never taught.

A few weeks into the job, in an examination room, I sat with a neuropsychologist for an entire workday as she tested a teenage cancer survivor. I took pages and pages of handwritten notes, jotting down the names of the tests she administered and the language she used to explain the tests to the patient. I watched the teen complete puzzles and answer questionnaires, take a lunch break and come back and do more. The room was small and cramped. I became a part of it, like a lamp or a painting hung on a clinic wall. When, hours into the day, the neuropsychologist asked me to share information about school accommodations, and I opened my mouth to ask to see a copy of the patient's school accommodation plan, my lips and tongue were dry and cottony from a day of quiet, focused watching. That was it, what I liked about my new work: I felt unusually focused. Sure, there's nearly nothing in the world as catastrophic as pediatric cancer, but I was energized by the shared purpose of the staff. It wasn't like my experiences teaching in elementary and high schools, where the teachers were always splitting off into new factions and cliques, often governed by who was buddies with what administrator, and where I hardly knew where I stood. I wondered if the cutting social dynamics rose out of a dearth of resources, because our city and state would never provide what we needed to make the education we provided humane. We didn't have what we needed in the public schools. The bathrooms didn't even have soap! The library had no librarian, just old, disorganized books on shelves, and no designated times for the kids to enter the space. You couldn't check anything out. The books were just there.

Every morning, I walked into the staff entrance of the hospital and got into a clean, working elevator. On every floor, there were millions of dollars' worth of supplies and personnel. I sat at my desk and made myself a neat to-do list. For the first time in my life, I thought, I wasn't being set up to fail. Maybe I could get good at a job and not feel like I was never doing enough.

When I am sent home, when my children are sent home, I begin cooking obsessively, in a way I never have before. Only in high school, when I was sick with an eating disorder, have I thought about food like this, much of the day, much of all days. I learned, years later, that some call this kind of thinking *food noise*.

It used to be that days carried different things. A Monday wasn't like a Thursday, and usually you knew the date offhand. On one day, you met a friend for drinks after work; on another, a kid had a soccer game; on the third, you had to drive two hours each way for your father's birthday dinner, at an Italian restaurant nestled on a quaint suburban downtown cul-de-sac, where you stressed over your kids' behavior in such a place.

The only thing that changes day to day now is the food that I make. Every meal could be the one that makes me feel better, couldn't it? I am trapped in a world of digital existence, and in that existence I find a group of digital women who want to teach me to be a better cook, a better baker.

I begin with Stella Parks. In her forty-six YouTube videos for *Serious Eats*, she teaches viewers to make classic, nostalgic American treats, as she did in her 2017 debut cookbook, *BraveTart: Iconic American Desserts*. With her, a pattern is set. A recipe is not enough: I need to watch her show me each ingredient, explain its importance, weigh it on a small digital scale. At a moment in which all I can watch is reruns of the same crime procedurals and spy shows I've already seen, Stella Parks videos are some of the only content that seem to penetrate.

After working in restaurants her whole young life, starting at fourteen, Parks became an editor at *Serious Eats*. Years before I knew what Slack or Zoom or Microsoft Teams were, Parks tested one to two dozen recipes at a time in her home in Lexington, Kentucky, commuting to Brooklyn for a week at a time when needed.

In a 2019 interview with Amy Madore, Parks admits, *It's still wild to me that* Serious Eats *is my full-time gig*. Kenji López-Alt hired Parks to write for *Serious Eats* after a Twitter discussion about a 1980s G.I. Joe PSA; Lopez sent her a DM, telling her he'd read her baking blog. When she began writing for López-Alt, before she was a full-time editor there, she received twenty-five dollars per *BraveTart* post. It wasn't a job, just a better place to write online, a place where more people might see her recipes, where she was part of a writing community.

In her video "How to Make Texas Sheet Cake," Parks, a shockingly pale, thin white woman, wears her signature dark eyeliner and dark-pink lipstick, high-waisted jeans, and T-shirt with flowers sprouting out of an ice cream cone. *This cake can serve anywhere between two and forty-five people, depending on how you cut it*, she says. *Or maybe just one.* She points at herself. *For me*, she mouths.

I could watch the video ten thousand times and I'd smile at this each and every time. This woman was named one of *Food & Wine* magazine's best new pastry chefs in 2012, six years before she made this video. A consummate restaurant professional. But what if this is what she's meant to do? What if reaching people like me is her calling? *I am her calling*, I think, standing in boxer shorts in my kitchen, hiding in the special spot the kids can't see from the living room. I am laughing alone at a woman I have never met baking a sheet cake in her imaginary kitchen.

Watching cooking videos seems like a good way to spend the time I used to spend commuting, socializing in the schoolyard, working out at the gym. By *good*, what I really mean is *productive*. I have never felt comfortable relaxing. Spending 8:01 watching Stella Parks make a homemade version of Klondike bars is great because we all love chocolate and ice cream, and now I have all the time in the world to make them at home. It could be good. I could be good.

But what of the 7:04 I spend watching Parks make blueberry pie? I don't like blueberries, and I don't like pie.

She is wearing a *Star Trek* T-shirt with a deeply swooped neck. She is wearing a brown belt with a big buckle. She says coriander and blueberry share an essential oil that improves the fruit's flavor. She uses the word *smooshing* to describe what she does to the edges of her beautiful lattice. She does this smooshing with fingers with imperfect gray nail polish. Did she do it herself, or has it just been on a while? Never in my life have I made pie crust that isn't either crumbly or greasy. There's alluring saxophone music playing when the pie goes into the oven. It's louder after the pie comes out. Nothing I know I wouldn't enjoy has ever looked so delicious. And now I've wasted over seven minutes, or, viewed through another lens, I am seven minutes closer to bedtime. Was seven minutes spent on the subway, in the hospital cafeteria at lunchtime, better spent? Would I still want to watch Stella Parks if she were knocking on doors, asking if anyone had seen anything, in a detective procedural?

Krys, what are you watching? a child asks, standing on the threshold between living room and kitchen. *A cooking video*, I answer every time.

I am done at the clinic. These days, my children are with me while I work. We eat breakfast and lunch and dinner together every day, at the same wooden table where two of them go to school and where I clock in and out of my job on a laptop. Nobody outside the family comes into our house for any reason. From our shared workspace, I email guidance counselors and teachers and parents and adolescent patients. There is a teenage patient I talk to twice a week, his parents chiming in from the background. *Now, I want you to fill out a Post-it note reminding you to finish your history homework. Stick it on the top of your computer screen. Next, make one for the math assignment you owe.* I speak these words confidently to the teen. But I am scared and lonely. I want to hear an adult's voice. Anna leaves for work in her scrubs, clutching her mask and her lunch bag, but the children and I always stay behind. Between meetings, I watch the older two in their little headphones. The kindergarten teacher is full of ideas about how to engage children through a computer screen, but let's be real, my son barely knows the sounds the letters make and spends half his time yelling, *Help! I pushed the wrong button!* He tries to get other family members to take his place in the Zoom Room, setting his device in front of the dog, in front of the cat, in front of his sister, who is only in preschool but is quickly picking up reading by attending kindergarten in her brother's place. One afternoon, the Chromebook is open and alone in the middle of our table. My son is perched in the upper corner of the doorframe, a miniature blond Spider-Man. The teacher calls out his name to figure out why he's disappeared. How did he get up there? *Nobody use the chat*, the second-grade teacher says to my other son's class, in a faraway, tinny voice. *I'm going to disable it if you don't stop!* In the next hour, I hear the speech therapist call his name: *Are you on another tab? Why are your eyes darting around the screen like that?*

The entirety of the Stella Parks YouTube oeuvre lasts approximately 198 minutes, without ad interruptions. So, of course, I watch the videos a second time. Days slide into other days, weeks slide into other weeks.

Parks excels most of all at very short videos, such as the forty-five-second "Homemade Cheez-Its." Set to whimsical music—I could imagine it being played on an amusement park ride, one that whips you around and presses you into the person next to you—the video has no voice-over. In my old life, I loved to send Anna to work with treats for her coworkers. There was something about looking like I did but being the one who knew how to cook and bake, at least, at the time, passably well. When I started, it was *My girlfriend made it*, and then it was *My wife made it*, and then *My partner made it. My partner made it, he's a really good baker.* I long for a time when you can make someone an impressive treat again. Sharing food outside your home has become the ultimate transgression.

Turns out a homemade version of Cheez-Its is pretty simple. By volume, there is more cheese than flour in Parks's recipe.

When she finished culinary school, Stella Parks had trouble finding a job. She returned home to Lexington from the Culinary Institute of America and *was just doing really advanced-level housekeeping. I was making crazy dinners for my husband and me and going to the farmer's market every day.*

I felt like I was wasting my time and my life, and there was an ever-growing gap on my résumé.

The first time I binge all her Serious Eats how-to videos over a few days' time ("How to Make Better Coffee Cake," "How to Make German Buttercream," this endless series of perfect desserts), I focus closely on all the things Parks can teach me. For example, in the Texas sheet cake video, she explains how it's primarily the fat content of fancy cocoa powders you order online that makes them taste better. She's the first person I notice telling viewers not just to scrape the bowl of their stand mixer while creaming butter and sugar at the beginning of a recipe but also to remove the beater and carefully scrape it, too, before adding other ingredients. *This has real-world ~~complications~~ implications*, she says, pushing through her flubbing of her own line. See? Her desserts are perfect, but she makes mistakes too.

Stella Parks sits in my food-content sweet spot. Because she is the first of the women I fall in love with on YouTube in these years, she comes to define my sweet spot. The room she cooks in is clearly a staged kitchen, not somewhere someone actually walks into in their bathrobe, groggy and irritable, to make morning coffee, not somewhere you'd drunkenly fry yourself an egg. But it also doesn't look professional, not like the places where she rose to prominence in a competitive field. So it's not home, but a home could theoretically get that clean and sparse, if all you did was clean and declutter all day, if you never let a child into your kitchen. It reminds me of visiting my parents' house, now that they're empty nesters, where the kitchen is much nicer than any kitchen I'll ever own or rent, and nobody ever uses any of the baking tins or the stand mixer. But in my parents' kitchen, the flour is five years old and the baking soda couldn't lift a cookie to save its life.

Stella Parks stands alone among exactly the ingredients she wants. It really is just her. She talks to me, not to the camera crew or to an assistant on set.

Parks has the look of someone put together, but not fancy, not dressed for a party, or in a chef's coat. It's like when you're meeting someone at a café and you make sure your favorite T-shirt is clean, that you find the right belt for this particular pair of pants. She makes things that, let's face it, you can also make out of various box mixes, but you won't—you want to make the turned-up version, not with any weird flavors or ingredients, just with lots of time and patience. Parks can talk you into using the right flour, the right cocoa powder, that scale that's been gathering dust in the cupboard, in the name of making something better.

The perfect walk with young children is achieved by satisfying a dual objective: one, to walk far enough to forget the inside of your home, the scattered toys and sink full of dishes; and two, to pick a destination not so far away that your children will tire before you make it there and back. Near our home in Philadelphia, that walk is to the produce store: nine blocks of varying lengths, past the school my children used to attend in person, past a square where many neighbors walk their dogs, mostly pit bulls and pit mixes with an occasional doodle or Great Dane mixed in, and where people in their twenties like to picnic and gather for yoga, past brick and stucco row homes, through the wide wooden door and into the market. Past the bags of heirloom beans and specialty goods in little jars and tins, the twelve-dollar boxes of imported Dutch cocoa powder, there is a bounty of local produce that is beyond worth the price. This isn't where I do our weekly shopping. Over the bridge, to the suburbs, I go once a week to load a cart with plastic-wrapped chicken and pork shoulder and ground beef, boxes of pasta and cereal and granola bars, gallons of milk and pounds of cheese. But for a bunch of herbs, a bag of apples, a selection of stone fruits to rip through in a day, sometimes just for the minutes we spend walking back home, this market is it. It is late May in the first of the plague years and I am walking with my children in tow. They are seven, six, and four years old.

Everyone in the market wears a mask, including me and my children. The kids sometimes smother me, but once we leave, I'm grateful to travel the world with a ready-made group. Along the back wall of the market, in the far-right-hand corner of the store, they have appeared: basket upon basket of fresh local strawberries. The berries are small and obscenely red, nestled one atop the next. There are things that still move me, I realize as I reach out to touch the first strawberry of the year that doesn't come to me in a hermetic plastic clamshell. These strawberries are vulnerable, unprotected. There are elements of the world that don't amount to fear or hatred or dread. Today can't be a cataclysmic error, not if I buy a few cartons of strawberries. The moment overwhelms me, in a nice way, not in the usual way. I owe it to my children to find these things that shake me awake. I grab two damp cardboard baskets of berries and send a kid over to the dairy case for a pint of heavy cream.

Sometimes, I think as we walk home talking about the planned dessert—scones sliced and topped with macerated strawberries and sweetened cream—you want something and then you get it. It's that simple. We walk home the nine blocks, masks on our chins, talking over one another about desserts. I hold a carton of strawberries in each hand. At the register, I declined a paper sack for our berries. I didn't want any of them to be crushed in the transfer. I wanted to walk home cradling them in my arms, like a baby.

I started making scones because I had mastered muffins of all kinds and realized that if I kept changing what I made, I could keep finding a reason to wake up and face another day. Recipes have come to feel like the most important thing in my world. The Stella Parks recipe is simple, and after I make it once or twice, I can make scones, start to finish, in half an hour. The original recipe calls for milk-chocolate chunks, but I start to vary the flavors, adding zests, making glazes. I rub butter into flour, stir in cream. Tonight, I'm making them for dessert. The strawberries wait for me in the refrigerator. While I listen to a physician's virtual lecture on a type of tumor that affects the eye, I make the scones plain, sprinkling turbinado sugar over the top before I bake them, maintaining focus on one simple fact: that after I am through learning the circumstances under which an oncologist might recommend enucleation of a child's cancerous eye, after I stare at one slide and another picturing the otherworldly glow of an optic nerve, I'll get to close the computer and make my family dessert.

In the blueberry pie video, the *Star Trek* T-shirt Stella Parks wears reads, *Darmok & Jalad at Tanagra*. It's a reference to season 5, episode 2 of *Star Trek: The Next Generation*, and this is my first introduction to the *Star Trek* universe. Anna is at the hospital and the kids are in bed and I am drinking a beer after another night of dinner and bathtime and bedtime and tidy time. I only sit down to watch television occasionally, because I only sit down occasionally.

The *Enterprise* makes contact with a Tamarian ship, and soon after, Captain Picard finds himself trapped by the Tamarian captain, Dathon, on an island. The two cannot communicate; Picard speaks simply and straightforwardly, while Dathon communicates elliptically, by telling stories from Tamarian legends and history.

While the *Enterprise*'s crew attempts to rescue Picard, they race to figure out the Tamarian language, which can't be accurately translated. Data says, *The Tamarian ego structure does not seem to allow what we normally think of as self-identity. Their ability to abstract is highly unusual. They seem to communicate through narrative imagery by reference to the individuals and places which appear in their mytho-historical accounts.*

Imagery is everything to the Tamarians, Troi remarks.

By wearing this specific T-shirt in her blueberry pie tutorial, Stella Parks is telling me something, something about the way cooking videos communicate through images. In the pie's tight double lattice, in the white subway tile of her test kitchen, in the matte gray of her polished nails, Parks is telling her audience who she is and what it would mean to listen to her.

In her *Star Trek* T-shirt, Stella Parks displays a complete bowl of berry filling. It's time to assemble.

I'm gonna grab the pie dough that I've previously made and rolled out and refrigerated for two hours, she says. She continues, comically, her explanation, because that's her job, isn't it, always overexplaining what it is she does with salt and flour and sugar and butter?

That helps it, Parks says,

. . . *be cold?*

There's a moment in the episode in which Picard and the Tamarian stand across a field shouting at each other. Dathon is calling out some Tamarian lore and Picard is totally missing the point. Dathon tosses a knife at Picard, who interprets this plea for teamwork as some sort of request for a duel. Everything about the show is campy, but this moment makes me feel, in my tired post-parenting-day state, weirdly bereft.

I am scared and angry and I don't understand how I am supposed to be the person and parent and partner I want to be. Every decision I make—whether it's safe to touch monkey bars, whether I should knock on the neighbor's door to share strawberry shortcake or just leave it on the stoop and retreat—is a maze of what-ifs. Reality is slipping away. My obsession with Stella Parks and the women like her, this gallery of popular cooking teachers, it's coming to be the only thing that makes sense. The food noise grows louder and louder and I begin to give in, to let it take over.

Stella Parks has a remarkable ability to look at a camera in a way that makes you feel she is looking at you. She's not on social media much, so these few hours of internet clips are all I have. I don't know why she chose the *Darmok & Jalad* shirt when she is the clearest communicator in my life.

In the comments on her brownie instructional video, YouTube user @matlit1859 writes, *Sometimes you get strong feelings that you can't explain. I had strong feelings when I saw the brownies being eaten with a glass of milk.*

I get strong feelings when I watch Stella Parks, when I watch her predecessors and her contemporaries and her successors, on the tiny laptop screen I put next to my cutting board each day. And I want to understand why.

Sara

I begin by trying to remember the first white woman who taught me to cook. As a teenager, I watched Sara Moulton because she was so smart about food. She often made accessible dishes on her shows, especially on *Sara's Secrets*, but her experience in restaurants and as a recipe editor and editor for *Gourmet* empowered her to explain why she did the things she did, as well as what was important to spend time and money on. I didn't shop for a family, and I only earned money here and there—first as a babysitter, and then as a teacher at the tae kwon do studio where I studied—so I couldn't go out and buy the things she named as she set up her mise en place, a phrase I learned from food television. When I walked to the grocery store between tae kwon do classes, I bought snacks: watermelon cubes in plastic containers, single-serving yogurts, boxes of six granola bars to keep in my backpack. But I was learning. I now knew how to mince a shallot, how to debone a chicken. By studying the way Moulton cooked her family-friendly dishes for *Cooking Live* and *Sara's Secrets*, I was preparing for a future I hadn't yet begun to imagine.

The house I grew up in was impossibly loud: my mother was loud, my five siblings were loud, the dogs, a series of golden and Labrador retrievers, were loud. First we were in a very small home, the downstairs of a duplex in which our bodies were always on top of one another, sitting in front of the window AC in the living room eating Firecracker Popsicles while our mother cooked yet another meal for the family, and then we were in a much larger, more echoey home, our mother's yelling reverberating off every wall. My mother treated food television as background fodder, something that was only half paid attention to. I learned from her that while you do the work of the home, you listen to the work of the home. Your life becomes a script you have to follow continuously in order to keep it working.

What was the adulthood I imagined? I hoped it wouldn't be this, this middle-aged drudgery my mother was in. There was a physical separation between her and any neighbor, between her and any other adult person. My parents lived in a wooded, bucolic suburb next to marshland. There weren't sidewalks, and if someone didn't live in a house we could get to by cutting through forests, we didn't hang out with them. I didn't understand why my parents had chosen this isolated place for our childhoods. I couldn't envision adulthood beyond my first job, figured maybe I'd just pop, like a balloon that had hit a tree branch. I didn't know any families I thought of as queer families growing up. I don't think I ever heard that word.

When I was thirteen, I won a writing contest and went to some workshops in New York, where, for the first time, I had freedom to wander on my own around a place with sidewalks. Putting one foot in front of another as I tried to navigate the blocks around the art gallery where the workshop would take place, I imagined what it would be like to be eighteen or twenty-three or twenty-nine. The edges were blurry, because I wasn't usually surrounded by people. Adult me sat on a couch. She sat at a desk. She was lonely, so she got a terrier. But when I was my mother's age, what could I be?

Like many teenagers, for all kinds of reasons, I felt trapped at home. I was grounded a lot, more than any of my friends, because my parents were stricter than theirs and because I've always had a smart mouth. If you'd told me at sixteen that in my thirties I'd mostly want to be at home, it would have sounded absurd. Home was the biggest trap of all.

Historian of queer domesticity Stephen Vider writes, in his book *The Queerness of Home*, that *while the home is not innately freeing, people of various identities and backgrounds have found emancipatory potential within the constraints.*

Vider's work complicates even my own impulse to dismiss domestic life as purely a series of conformities, a way of shrinking myself into an expected narrative. Vider looks at the ways queers experimented with the idea of the domestic sphere in the decades after World War II, analyzing, among many other things, what the meaning of home could be in a queer context. Though we could take it in new directions, and though many did, we were still in some ways bound by the ideas of family and home that existed outside queer community.

Social inclusion, within the family, the community, and the nation, Vider writes, *all depend on performing domesticity correctly, that is, following the scripts of the white, middle-class, heterosexual home.*

The script was that every morning my mother got up and turned on the coffeepot, that she made breakfast for the kids who were too little to make it themselves, that while we all went somewhere—us to school, my father to work—she cleaned the house up and down, did the laundry, bought the groceries, took my father's suits to the dry cleaner, and then she picked us up from school, took us to sports, made us all dinner, and cleaned up after the nightly disaster that was six children eating and doing homework and showering and going off to bed. My mother loved babies and toddlers, the work of that, the breastfeeding and soothing and rocking, and I'm not saying she didn't love us once we were older, but we exhausted and exasperated her, anyone could see that. Every August, my mother brought the six of us to a stuffy strip mall for new sneakers we would bring home in boxes, place in our closets, and avoid wearing till the first day of school. One by one, we would sit on a bench and get measured, and after our turn was up and we'd lifted our sole off the long metal foot-shaped ruler, we'd act bad, I mean horrible, running though she'd reminded us, *Don't run!*, asking for shoes that were more expensive than the budget we'd been assigned, fistfighting over who was going to get what. I can't remember my father ever taking us to do something so existentially mundane and terrible as back-to-school shoe shopping.

His script took place outside the house. He went to work: long hours, trips abroad. He coached T-ball and basketball. When he was home, he installed things, or organized things, or delegated the organizing of things out to us. And okay, none of that is easy, but none of it is daily, either, other than the paid work. I didn't want to be a stay-at-home mom, but I'm not sure, if someone had offered me a replica of my father's life, I'd have wanted that either.

I didn't like the way my parents' power dynamics played out. They fought over money and who was more tired or deserved or didn't deserve leisure. My mother's main power was in her voice, because the family money was hers but also not. Their relationship felt equal in some senses, but what my mother would do in an emergency was never clear to me. It seemed distinctly scary and unromantic in a gendered kind of a way. There was and is a sense of love, but love tied up in so much else.

In recent decades, Vider notes, families like my parents' have become steadily less common, with fewer houses comprised of married cishet couples, with increasing numbers of Americans, including many older people, living alone. Still, Vider notes, the dream is there, and *the vision of the romantic couple has continued to hold sway in popular culture and the law as the surest path to personal happiness and national belonging.*

When you watch a celebrity television chef, you mostly watch them alone.

Just like I liked watching the women on television, I liked watching my mother make the actual meals that fed our family, every single breakfast and lunch and dinner, except for occasional delivered pizza or trips to Chili's or Macaroni Grill, or Friendly's when my dad was out of town.

One of my mother's favorite shows was Rachael Ray's *30 Minute Meals*, which aired the year I was in the eighth grade. The show featured a frenzied series of actions: Ray literally ran back and forth from her cupboard to grab bags of pasta or grains, furiously patted meat dry with paper towels, opened giant cans, her forearms straining with the speed of it all. And the whole time, she talked, in an almost pressured way, about what she was doing.

I liked that my mother, who grew up in a home with no good cooks and not enough money, also chattered the entire time she prepared food. She talked at us about people who lived on our cul-de-sac in stiff colonial houses like ours; she caught up with friends and family with the cordless phone tucked under her chin; sometimes, she talked quietly to herself, narrating the steps of whatever she was making. Making meals every day for so many people had made a cook out of her. My mother poured vegetable oil and vinegar and a packet of dressing mix into a glass bottle and shook it vigorously. She took off her rings to mix meat and breadcrumbs and spices in a big bowl. She roasted potatoes in a giant baking dish. She cut red onions into bits with a steak knife. She breaded chicken cutlet after chicken cutlet after chicken cutlet and the whole time, she talked incessantly, at me, at anyone in the room, at the dog, sometimes at nobody.

In *Watching What We Eat: The Evolution of Television Cooking Shows*, Kathleen Collins distinguishes Sara Moulton from Ray: *Though Moulton was a bit breathless and rushed at times in her hour-long show, it was not the choreographed spectacle that Rachael Ray performs in* 30 Minute Meals.

Realism is a key element of the Moulton universe. Watching *Cooking Live*, a home cook can literally cook along with Moulton, who begins with all raw ingredients and has at them methodically while explaining the work she is doing.

As an adult, I watch Moulton, observing how even when she is fishing around unproductively for a kitchen implement, her very being is suffused with calm.

In an interview with food journalist Benjamin Kemper, Moulton explains her passion for teaching home cooks: *Both my husband and I grew up with dinner on the table every night. It's my religion.*

I found myself always looking for that Moulton energy, the focused calm no one in my family or life seemed to have. I felt it come over me in the Barnes & Noble on Route 17 near my parents' house in Bergen County, New Jersey. The books I most coveted were on the perimeter, along the wall that separated the gigantic main bookstore from the used section at the back end of the store. They had put the small selection of gay books—I don't remember what they were called then, before the acronyms started growing, before the workers at a quiet suburban shop would have plastered the word *QUEER* on a shelf—next to sections with religious books. I felt at home there, too, amid the Christian iconography. As a young child, I had read the collected short biographical sketches of the saints more than any other book. I read it mostly in the bathroom, where it lived in a wicker basket balanced on the back of the toilet. There was something romantic, almost erotic, about some of the saints' lives. These men and women, they did things. Big things. They were martyrs and iconoclasts. They had been ordinary and then they were not. What child doesn't long for such a thing? It was queer, in a way, their defiance and their radical, mysterious acts.

Barnes & Noble was the one place open late that I liked to go. It closed at ten on the weekends. After dinner, I could drive to the bookstore and be around people but avoid interacting with any of them. Sure, there were friends who would invite me to their parties or over to their houses, but none of those spaces, those groups of teenage girls, felt quite right to me. There was a specific cafeteria table at school where lesbians sat, but I was afraid to talk to them, though they all knew me and I knew them. Speaking to someone one-on-one, sitting next to them in class, that was very different from joining the group, even just for one lunch—the whole school would see, would look at you. You couldn't break bread with those people consequence-free.

Sara Moulton's debut cookbook is the first one I remember seeing on the shelf there in the big bookstore where I went to be away from my family. On the cover of *Sara Moulton Cooks at Home*, she wears a modest blue scoop-neck shirt and an orange apron. She holds a tangled bundle of asparagus in her arms.

The apron is emblazoned with the logo for her show: *sara's secrets*, it says, humbly, in lowercase blocky print.

In the context of the show, a *secret* is something that can only be good, a tip that will transform the drudgery of shopping and prepping and cooking and plating your food into an unexpectedly transcendent experience. Sara Moulton shared secrets with me like I was her friend, though of course I knew we would never meet. I remember the first time I started to admit it to myself. Not that I was a guy, just that I wasn't the thing I was expected to be. I was walking alone in the woods, having been dropped off by my school bus. I was wearing my plaid kilt and my green knee socks. I was in the early stages of recovery from anorexia, so nothing fit, it all billowed around me in the wind. I didn't like my body. I didn't like food. I didn't like that to get home from the bus I had to cut through strangers' yards. As lonely as I was, the last thing I wanted was for someone to look out their back window and see me moving toward the home where, though it was a kind of home, I knew I could never be myself. I was listening to music on a big classic iPod. I was sixteen years old. Old brown leaves crunched under my feet. The new ones were just coming in all around me, the forest a loose, shy green. *I'm gay*, I whispered, to absolutely no one.

On *Cooking Live*, Sara Moulton wears chef's coats. They look trim and professional on her small, compact body. Moulton told *Cape Cod Times* reporter Laurie Higgins in 2007 that when, in the 1970s, she heard men talking about how women could not be successful in the kitchen, *That was catnip to me. I'm a short female and I have a Napoleon complex. If you tell me I can't do it, I will do it.* She wears a blond ponytail and looks like a professional athlete, the kitchen her playing field. She has great bangs. She travels around the kitchen confidently, like she's following preset plays. Not many clips from this show remain on the internet, but when I watch them as a thirtysomething man, I notice things I didn't remember but am certain I noticed as a child: the big, rolled-up sleeves on her blue chef's coat, her sporty hairdo, her natural, if present at all, makeup.

I didn't know people could transition until I was seventeen years old. I didn't learn it from one of the books I read in secret along the back wall of the bookstore. I learned it from a LiveJournal kept by someone I started college with, a trans man who seemed extremely boring and dorky in some ways but unbelievably radical in others. He was just some guy! It was wild. I know this is all weird, because I grew up where I did, and went to high school in the aughts, and could see the New York City skyline on my way to high school, down Route 17, but this just wasn't a thing I'd heard of before college. *Lesbian* was the end of the queer road in my parochial high school. So when I looked for models of the kind of adult I could be, I looked for women with haircuts like Moulton's, practical women, women who, because of their professions, had to wear sensible shoes at all times. Whether the woman on the screen was gay or not, that didn't matter. What mattered was finding models of success whose costumes looked like something I could stomach wearing.

Moulton has had a long career as a public conveyer of food wisdom. In the mid-1980s, she began her public food work, editing at *Gourmet*, and continued on to work at *Good Morning America* and on Food Network. Higgins notes in her profile of Moulton that she had been working as a sous-chef at La Tulipe, a French bistro in the West Village, but was at the point in her life where she wanted to have children and knew she couldn't do that while working eighty hours a week in a restaurant. It's not that I don't believe Moulton conveyed this sentiment to Higgins, or to whomever led her Wikipedia entry to say the same—*In the interest of starting a family, she left restaurant work and began devoting herself instead to recipe testing and development*—but I keep looking for a direct quote and coming up empty. Why do I feel I need to hear her say it herself?

When did the desire for family life start to seep into my own? There isn't a time I remember when my mother wasn't mothering at least one child other than me. Feeding us took up an enormous amount of her time. We were the work of her life. My mother never pressured me to have children. Nobody wants or expects queers to do it. Of course, it's only in retrospect that I understand I was a queer child. I didn't know what that was. All I knew was that whatever my mother had, this life of cooking and cleaning, didn't seem like something I was supposed to want, supposed to get.

The secrets of *Sara's Secrets* are slightly elevated versions of things I grew up eating in our Wonder Bread–white American kitchen. In this way, the show is an extension of Moulton's previous work demystifying the actions a woman performs in her kitchen. In her *Cooking Live* episode simply titled "Burgers," Moulton speaks authoritatively but casually about ground lamb, an ingredient many American home cooks twenty years ago might have found unusual. She explains how to ask a butcher for the best grind but acknowledges that interacting with a butcher is something a lot of us don't get to do, bound to the shrink-wrap of the supermarket as we are.

She speaks in relatable aphorisms. *Take it home, season it, cook it right up, you're in business.*

Sara Moulton is a good teacher. She knows how to explain techniques and ingredients in a way that both beginners and more seasoned cooks understand. If she thinks an ingredient might not be at the Pathmark or whatever store you frequent, she tells you where to get it. In a fifty-five-minute episode, she makes three different burgers—a lamb patty served in a pita, a chili cheeseburger, and a tuna burger.

Like my mother, I do most of my cooking for young children, and for a partner who grew up in a part of the world without much variety at the market. Anna describes bread lines, root vegetables. Sometimes I try something new, but over the years, I've gotten into predictable patterns and routines. I have my go-tos. I have learned that the most likely successes in the kitchen, when you're cooking for your family, are slight variations on meals they already like. Thus, something like what Moulton is doing, making a sandwich that looks like a basic hamburger, that is called a burger, is almost guaranteed to work.

Sitting at a table with three gigantic dressed burgers and a modest glass of wine, Sara Moulton concludes the episode by answering questions from her fans.

This is where Moulton, like any great teacher, shines: responding to these queries with care and automaticity. She still does this on a weekly basis, on Christopher Kimball's podcast *Milk Street Radio*. Moulton and Kimball, the cofounder and former host of *America's Test Kitchen*, take questions from home cooks. Listeners call in with all kinds of queries, but the ones I like best are from people trying to reconstruct family recipes. The callers describe what a cake looked like and tasted like, and Moulton and Kimball offer advice on resurrecting a dormant, grandmotherly joy.

In one episode, a caller named Jerry from Vermont describes his family's annual viewing of the 1983 made-for-TV holiday film *The Gift of Love: A Christmas Story*. In one scene, Jerry relates, *Angela Lansbury's character proclaims that she is going to make her famous burnt orange cake. What could that be?* Jerry wants to know.

Wow, Moulton says. *I've never heard of this before, though it sounds absolutely wonderful.* The first thing she says to someone on this podcast is always a version of the same thing. I hear you, I care about what you said, I care about your cooking. Though Christopher Kimball, a significantly drier and more pedantic teacher, says he believes the burnt orange refers to the color of the cake, Moulton seems caught up in the delight of the question and its ascendant possibilities. *I envision*, she says, *a wonderful orange cake that you then pour a dark caramel syrup over, and just let it infuse.*

Jerry likes this idea, he says.

Nobody transcribes these episodes, so I don't know how to spell the question-asker's name. I suppose I've chosen Jerry with a *J* to distance him from Gerry with a *G*, my father, who rarely prepared food for the family, though on the rare occasions he did, he turned out to be quite skilled in the kitchen.

When I arrived at college, I met a young man from an East Coast suburb who seemed to have no qualms about telling peers he had four mothers. As a young child, he'd had two, and then they divorced and each remarried. The town where he grew up was probably much like mine, and he likely had friends similar to my brothers: white boys who enjoyed lab sciences and played varsity sports. We weren't even friends; he was just someone who dated a girl in my residence hall. But hearing about his family of mothers, I gathered you could get to a point where having a family like that could be regular, could exist without all the throat clearing and justifying. And in a way, I was jealous, not only of the ease with which this stranger talked about his queer family but also with the sheer number of mothers he had to choose from. So if one gave bad advice, he could ask another? If one yelled too much while he was sitting at the kitchen counter, he could leave the room and go into the den, where he might be met by a different, quieter mother? I had spent much of my early teenage years looking for replacement mothers, for people who would speak kindly to me. *I hear you, I care about what you said*, that sort of a thing. Sometimes I developed twisted, confusing crushes on them, and other times, I just wanted them to offer me a ride home and ask me what books I was reading or talk to me about anything other than how I really had to get going on cleaning my room, or organizing my closet, or paying my library fines, or clearing out the crumpled paper collection at the bottom of my backpack. There wasn't anything wrong with the mother I had, who made amazing pasta with red sauce, who gave me the endpiece of the meat loaf, who had the formidable arm strength to mash enough potatoes so we could eat as many helpings at dinner as we wanted. She loved us, but not in the slow way of a woman who pays attention to you. She was a blur of movement and service. What if I had four?

What I like about the dream of a burnt orange cake is the imagination in it: you take the rawest of materials, a man you've never met talking about a cake from a movie, a cake that's never shown or discussed in great detail in said movie, and you construct something beautiful out of it, and you share that creation. My family gave me these raw materials: a father at work, a mother in the kitchen, me and my siblings, raised with love but not with affection, demanded upon to perform in school and on athletic fields. And as a girl, and the oldest, I had to do more chores, sure, and I had to care for my siblings. When my youngest sister was born, I was thirteen. In photos, I hold her like someone who's been doing it his whole life, cradling other people. When Anna and I had our first child, she seemed amazed by my facility at handling a newborn, at withstanding the crazy-making labor of it. He cried all the time and I was just fine with it, integrated his noise into the life I was living. She had birthed him, our first son, who looks just like her, and who was conceived with a friend's sperm. Real twenty-first-century shit. But the actions were the same ones I knew from when I was young. When our son woke up at night, I stood next to the crib and rocked him, looking out at the faint glow of the lamps along Locust Avenue. A few months later, I sat him down and handed him a thick apple slice, the first food he would taste. And I took a picture of his tongue hitting the apple's flesh.

Sometimes you think you're making something new, but really you're just doing the same thing you've been doing your whole life.

In the 2022 interview with Benjamin Kemper, Sara Moulton is asked about the gender divide in cooking—those who light things on fire (Emeril Lagasse, Bobby Flay) versus those who help Mom get dinner on the table. Moulton answers flatly on the dynamics of early cable food television: *They didn't really want women at Food Network.*

Cooking Live ran for an astounding 1,200-plus episodes. All those days and nights of new ideas for us home cooks. *Sara's Secrets* came next and ran for just three years. After that, Moulton moved on from Food Network, onto American Public Television. On *Sara's Secrets*, Moulton dresses differently than she had before. She ditches the chef's coat. She wears what my stay-at-home mother wore: basic slacks and workmanlike long-sleeve T-shirts, tight on the whole body, covered by plain aprons. She is presented, then, as a regular person, not a professional, cooking on a homey set in front of some windows. There's something more feminine about her presentation here, though I am not sure *feminine* is the right word, and I don't consider Moulton to be in a certain category among hot white woman television chefs—Claire Robinson of *5 Ingredient Fix*, Katie Lee of *The Kitchen* and *Beach Bites with Katie Lee*—all, perhaps, Nigella Lawson derivatives in their own ways. The long-sleeve tees, though, lack the gender ambiguity of a loose-fitting chef's coat. Of all the items of clothing in the world, it was a tight girls' T-shirt that gave me the most trouble growing up, the way it clung to me.

On an episode of *Sara's Weeknight Meals*, which first aired on American Public Television in 2008, Moulton tells us she is going to be making vegan food, while carrying a rustic-looking basket of potatoes out of a pantry closet. The television home is cluttered in a lived-in way, with sunflowers poking out of a large pot. You can see a cracked-open door to the bathroom, which implies that this house extends beyond the kitchen into other rooms. It's one of the few television kitchen sets that gestures toward a larger house, where the family watches TV or plays video games or does homework in other rooms as they wait for the meal you are making. But you never get a full view of the other rooms. This isn't Moulton's actual home. She acknowledges this in a 2022 interview: *We shot at my producer's partner's house in Greenwich, in full disclosure, which is where we pretend it's my home, which is nicer looking than my home here in New York City*. There's a way in which the success of the gentle weeknight mom depends on this set, this generic, non-urban-looking home. Some nights in Philadelphia, I do dream of cooking in somebody else's house, but without good reason. We have an unusually large kitchen for the neighborhood. It was, like many of the non-tiny kitchens of Kensington, built onto the back of the house, possibly without a permit, possibly in a way that eliminates the possibility of ever building on top of it. Even though our house isn't tiny, it is cramped with all of us living in it. Things that go outside, like bicycles, helmets, and the like, need to have places on the inside, given the lack of garage or shed and the propensity of anything left outside to wander off for street resale.

In her thousands of television episodes, Moulton has cooked a dizzying variety of foods. The woman can cook anything. But she spotlights other cooks when she can. The first time she appears on-screen with Adam Sobel in the vegan cooking episode, she touches his back gently as if they are in her home together, as if he is her friend, even her child. While he slices tofu into thin strips for what he calls Korean BBQ Tofu Tacos, she explains for her audience what tofu is. She pronounces the word with an emphasis on the *fu*, and pronounces *marinade* with a French intonation, before correcting herself quickly, turning the short *a* into a long one. She stands next to him, questioning him, narrating what he's doing, pointing, and leaning in very closely. Sometimes her hands are in his space, but she restrains herself from, for example, taking the knife out of his hands to show him how she would do it. *Let me tell you about, um, a little trick I have*, she says, like someone who can't stop herself from sharing. She describes saving leftover tofu by freezing it, noting that it's more absorbent after it's thawed. Sobel explains what freezing does to the proteins. He has a spark of something—in montages of his cooking and working with the staff of his food truck, the Cinnamon Snail, he has the faux-casual air of a talented guitarist in a grunge band or a national Frisbee champion. Though he will continue to have a career in food, he will not go on to a long and celebrated television career. He'll never touch Moulton's fame.

I've been teaching now for much of my life. First, it was Irish dancing, which I taught to young children in exchange for tuition. Then, it was tae kwon do, which I taught in a strip mall studio as a teen. After that, tennis basics with a local Special Olympics squad. In college, a similar program, a disabled soccer mentorship. And then I began my classroom teaching: high school, elementary school, college, online writing classes. You learn, when you're teaching, that it doesn't matter who you are, how sure you are. There are simply fundamentals to the work, the onion chopping of getting a stranger to listen to and learn from you.

In the Kemper interview, Moulton recalls cooking her first meal on a solo television spot. Cooking on one's own is markedly different from cooking with a host, she tells Kemper. *For my pilot I cooked fish meunière and asparagus—and never once smiled.*

Don't smile until Christmas, the popular teaching adage goes.

Hi, I said on my first day teaching high school. I was twenty-one years old. *I'm Ms. McIlraith*, I said brightly. I wore loose slacks and a button-down shirt. A tie would have been a bridge too far, I thought.

Of course, I could not help it—I smiled at my students.

We'll have you out by November, someone said from the back of the classroom.

Food Network wasn't, in Moulton's early years, what it became. Network executives weren't hiring performers. They were hiring chefs. Moulton existed just on the cusp. After her first experience cooking on television alone—*I held up the asparagus to show what it should look like and it was waving around in the air because my hands were shaking so much*—the network set her up with media training. Prodded by her trainer to figure out the reason why she should be on TV, Moulton remembered that she's a good teacher. She tells Collins, *That's the one thing I can say and brag about and pound my fists on my chest and say, "I'm a great teacher."*

Bridget and Julia

I like to watch Anna's mouth when she talks, and when she laughs, and when she eats. Anna has big teeth and thin, freckled lips. If I close my eyes, I can place exactly each of the four freckles. I first kissed Anna when I was nineteen years old. Soon after, I made her dinner for the first time. At the co-op in town, I purchased a sackful of fresh vegetables and some pasta, which I carried back to my dormitory on the edge of campus. I wanted to make her something easy and fresh.

In the dorm kitchen, which basically no one used, I stood with my back to her and cooked dinner. She was my first girlfriend, my first anything. *You know I like you, right?* she'd said, sitting with me during a movie screening that our rugby team had hosted on a Friday night, to keep us away from campus parties. *What? No*, I'd said. She'd left a seat between us, sensing I might not want her any closer. The first time, she kissed me on the cheek, then the mouth, because she knew it would scare me a little, being touched. Before that night in the dorm kitchen, I'd never cooked for someone who wasn't in my family.

With something to do, with spots I had to occupy—the spot at the counter, where I did the prep, the spot at the stove, where I sautéed the vegetables, the spot at the sink, where I drained the pasta and washed the dishes—I found I could listen, really listen, to what Anna was saying, better than when we were sitting together. Without movement, I felt pressured to move and speak the right way, in a way that made me seem calmer and more attentive than I was. I was funnier, too, quicker with a quip while snapping woody ends off stalks of asparagus. Anna talked fast, and when she was tired, her accent came out, and she mixed up vowels, because so many of English's vowel sounds don't exist in Polish, her first language, and there were essential things she said that I worried I was missing. I wanted her to think I could pay attention. With my body making small, assigned movements—hands peeling garlic cloves, salting pasta water, turning spaghetti strands—I was present. I was the person she had pined for across the rugby pitch, a blur of movement and purpose. In motion, I didn't think about what I looked like, what that meant. When, after sex, Anna would stare at my face too long, I would get self-conscious. She was falling in love with a woman's face. Something in me had thought that dating someone, creating the world of a relationship, would help me feel more like I belonged in the world, but it was only such a small step toward feeling normal. I still felt paralyzed. Small decisions—the classes I registered for each semester, the people I dated, the jobs I applied for—those I could make, but the truth was that I knew I was letting the wrong adulthood keep flowing at and through me, failing to make the big decisions that would have been necessary to change the kind of life I could live.

At the chipped, institutional, college-owned kitchen in Palmer Hall, I took my time plating our pasta. Anna didn't have a lot of money, so she didn't eat out much, never had. I wanted to give her something that tasted better than what we were used to in the dining hall. Facing away, I lingered at the counter, grating a pile of cheese with the dorm's dull box grater. I felt Anna's gaze lingering on the back of me, on my athlete's body, trim and androgynous, muscled calves, round ass. The idea of someone watching me cook was an unexpected turn-on.

We sat down to eat, away from everyone else on earth. I watched her mouth move, watched her get up to serve herself seconds. It made me proud, making someone else happy this way.

One of my enduring memories from those earliest days, before I would have considered us serious, before we owned anything together, when we were so young and not yet out to our families and unpracticed at being queer in the world, and always on the verge of ending things for one reason or another, I told Anna that even if we broke up, I would find her, wherever life had taken her, and I would bake her children birthday cupcakes to take to school because she did not think that was something she could manage, even if she used a box mix.

Never, in the years before we had children, did we talk about who would make our dinners. I make dinner every night because I want to, and because I need to. Other people want and need me to. When Anna is home, I get to take my time, pulling out more cutting boards and bowls, maybe even the food processor or the stand mixer, making sauces and condiments and garnishes. A bowl of slow-fried shallots, an aioli, a sharp vinaigrette. Those nights I make simple desserts, brownies or cookies or a single-layer cake with a glaze. I go the extra mile: brown the butter, toast the nuts, make fresh rolls.

When Anna isn't home, when she's at work and I have all the kids to feed and get to bed on my own, I cook as fast as I can: quesadillas stuffed with leftovers, grilled cheeses with sliced apples, one-pot pastas, sheet pan pancakes cut into giant rectangles with the pizza cutter, fried egg sandwiches, bagel melts, snack plates. I am trying to get one thing done so I can move on to the next. While the kids eat, I clean, scrubbing my cutting board, wrapping cheddar in plastic wrap to go back in the fridge. I toss, literally toss, fun-size candy bars across the counter for the kids to have as an after-dinner treat. Then, I shoo them away from their places so I can wipe everything down and get them to bed.

Stephen Vider, the historian of queer domesticity, tracks the ways in which within the movement for gay and lesbian rights and its manifestation in public and private, the home represents a fraught space. His wide-ranging examination of public and political messaging and cultural artifacts from and about queer private life articulate something at the core of my daily labor. *The underlying perversity of home*, Vider writes, *is that it operates simultaneously as a site of agency and constraint: the romance of home as a site of self-expression, intimacy, and autonomy depends on the constraints it imposes.*

Sometimes it feels like I have experienced much of my thirty-eight years on earth as a series of failures. I was good at reading and writing but I was not the best student, always lost in maelstroms of crumpled papers and quarter-filled notebooks. I was aloof and difficult and messy at home. I have failed to maintain many friendships, and I've never stayed at any job longer than two years, eleven months. I failed to be straight. I failed to be a girl.

In cooking, I have found a series of guarantees, some of my only successes. Ice cream out of your own machine always tastes better than anything store-bought, even if the recipe isn't anything special, even if it's just cream and milk and sugar you pour into a machine before hitting *Go*. If you make a baked pasta dish, people will be happy. If you put a pork shoulder in the oven on a very low temperature, your day will accumulate into a triumph of melted fat and amazing smells. That is the promise of *America's Test Kitchen*: they had the failures so you can have the successes. I don't want a recipe to break the world open. In getting my family fed, all I want is a series of easy wins.

The promise of food instruction is that it can make the food better, or it can it make cooking dinner every day, every single day, easier, or sometimes both. While I cook and while I clean, my second son joins me at the counter. Unlike our other children, who are gangly and thin, like their mother, this son is solid, muscled and blocky. He is an athlete and an enthusiastic eater. He is, in some ways, like a second me. He leans his elbows to watch our current favorite: old episodes of *America's Test Kitchen.*

Finally, after running through every free episode I can find online, I decide to pony up $79.99 annually for an all-access online subscription to *Cook's Illustrated*, *Cook's Country*, and *America's Test Kitchen*. For that money, I get access to their recipe archives, equipment reviews, and videos. I cook from their archives a good deal—they have dependable recipes for almost anything I'd want to make. There are some regulars: spicy pork noodles with Szechuan peppercorns; tomatoey ground beef tacos the kids love; cream drop biscuits into which I put chives, scallions, cheddar cheese, spices, and chilis; the best and most labor-intensive oatmeal muffins I can imagine—you have to toast oats in butter and then grind them into oat flour before you begin, but I do it, and you should too, because the muffins are that good, perfect for a morning when the kids get up earlier than expected. Mostly I look at their recipes to get ideas about ratios, flavor combinations. I read and trust their product reviews. Anna and I select their recommended five-cup automatic Zojirushi coffee maker when, finally facing down too many daily kitchen tasks, I store the grinder and french press in a cabinet. For years, I clung to the ritual, the timer ticking down as the coffee steeped, but eventually Anna and I came to bemoan the longest four minutes of our lives, and we had to admit our life had defeated the ritual, and with it, in a way, the people we thought ourselves to be.

America's Test Kitchen has been posting episodes of their show on YouTube for years. They were my bridge off traditional television—I started watching their clips and episodes before I found Serious Eats and Bon Appétit and their many spinoffs, before *The New York Times* began collecting and creating food entities beyond Mark Bittman and Melissa Clark, before Instagram was video based and cooking videos began invading my phone too. I liked that I could put my laptop on the counter and cook along, that I could fast-forward and rewind and pause as much as I wanted, much easier than on our family's one television, which was in a different room, and only has a working remote about 50 percent of the time. I liked that online food programming didn't have the artifice of plot, and I liked that there was no live audience. I was the audience.

Central to *America's Test Kitchen* is cooking instruction in which one cook teaches not the audience but another cook to make a dish. Instead of explaining to the camera why corn syrup works better in the dessert than granulated sugar would, or what mixing baking soda into a ground meat will do to its browning, the cook explains to someone standing right next to them. Sometimes the observer is turned into an observer-participant, given small tasks such as stirring a pot while the teacher chops vegetables off to the side, but as the audience, we're meant to understand that a second person isn't necessary to the dish's completion. They're there to learn, and, more importantly, to taste.

In the video in which Bridget Lancaster makes pecan sticky buns and Julia Collin Davison watches, the women stand inches apart as Bridget pats and nudges and pulls the dough into a rectangle with unbelievable tenderness and care. They are middle-aged blond white women who have been making episodes like this one for years. They laugh like there's no camera, like they're in one of their home kitchens, though unlike some other food television, the set of *America's Test Kitchen* centers the test part of the equation—it's clear many people work on recipes all day in this place. Between shots, the camera pans out occasionally to a crowded, many-stationed kitchen, a lab of sorts, but when Bridget and Julia are demonstrating, the camera zooms in, focuses just on them.

Julia stares as Bridget touches and touches and touches the dough. *You look like you're in the dough zone*, Julia quips, and the women laugh.

This is very meditative, Bridget says, pushing a brown sugar filling out to the edges of her eighteen-by-fifteen-inch enriched dough rectangle.

The women are not touching, but they are so close that one's arm overlaps the other's. I get into those states too, trance-like, peeling chickpeas for hummus, spreading frosting on a cake, and it's strangely erotic to watch someone watching someone in that place.

It's like a Zen sand garden, Julia says, and Bridget digs the analogy.

There's a pause.

I love cooking with you, Bridget says.

Part of me feels silly even bringing this lens onto them. Maybe there's nothing queer about any of this. But I love to watch them, and the physical chemistry is part of it.

My perception is perhaps warped from decades of feeling like there is a palpable barrier between me and everyone else that begins inches, even a foot or more, from my body.

Unlike any Black or Brown man, or a white man with a dirt-stained work uniform and lunch cooler, or any man who looks like he doesn't have a place to stay, I am not intimidating or ominous to strangers. I'm just repellant in a way I can't quite lay down. A tiny white guy in a denim jacket and sneakers. There's an otherness I thought transition would change completely, but it didn't. Being a man didn't change the fact that other people do not want to be near me, do not want to touch me, do not want to look at me.

This is why, in that classroom where our rugby team watched Miranda July's *Me and You and Everyone We Know*, I was surprised—like mouth-hanging-open-for-real surprised—when Anna told me she was into me. My body felt like something not fully understood, not yet animated by the same things that animated others. How could someone desire something so pre-realized? College was part of the unreality. We slept in rooms that were not parts of homes, and we ate all our meals in a place that was attached to but was not itself a kitchen. In July's film, a strange, artsy white woman falls in love with a boring white shoe salesman who has two biracial Black children. In an early scene, the man is talking to his children in their room. He has only recently come to live in this bachelor's apartment. *At Mom's house, we have a chore wheel*, the younger child says. He explains how it works: *You put chores on it and then you can spin it. There's this metal thing . . . and it helps it to spin. It's spinning from the metal.*

Of course, I cannot say what Anna and I were thinking in 2006 as we watched this film, an empty seat between us. Imposing what I know now on the watching, she regards the strange, disconcertingly forthcoming, thin brunette artist with a mixture of recognition and longing. If she had turned another way, she could be alone in an apartment recording strange artistic videos. That sort of thing is, after all, what some of her peers in the theater department went on to do.

There is a scene in the film in which the woman, enamored with the shoe salesman, opens up his passenger door and slips into his car. They had just shared an unsettlingly intimate moment on the street outside the department store where he works. When they separate, she looks back and he does not. In his car, sunlight streams through his windows, highlighting his smile and then the settled, satisfied look he gets when the rush of the interaction passes.

But the woman changes her mind about the separation and chases after his car. She suggests he drive to her car, and then steps inside.

He's not pleased.

What are you doing in my car?

She laughs uncomfortably.

I don't know you, and you certainly don't know anything about me. What if I'm . . . a killer of children?

Well, that would put a damper on things, wouldn't it? she says.

You're acting like I'm just a regular man, he says. *Like a man in a book who the woman in the book meets.*

The implication, I suppose, is that whatever she thinks she's seeing in him, he is so much more, both in good and bad ways.

I had chosen the movie that night. I told the women on my rugby team, *This might get weird.*

I was nineteen. I was a sophomore at an elite/ist college. I probably wasn't going to live in a dumpy apartment or work in a shoe store. Marriage, kids, separation, these were faraway concepts to me. And yet this man rose back to top of mind, when Anna said we should try being together.

You're acting like I'm just a regular man.

I told her to give me a week to think about it.

There's something about watching people who have a tension like that, a complicated semi-sexual tension. Julia Collin Davison and Bridget Lancaster appear together in dozens, perhaps hundreds, of video clips. Superimposed on the teaser image of every video from 2019's season 18 is a picture of Lancaster with her arm atop Collin Davison's shoulder. They look intimate, but tough. I watch the videos in a trance: in their demonstration of a one-pot, four-ingredient macaroni and cheese, Julia talks about innovations to the recipe while the two lock in intense eye contact. They stand close together and laugh together at things that aren't quite funny. I feel like I'm seeing a workplace romance happen on-screen.

Of course, it's not a good idea for teammates to fuck, but everyone knows this is just how queers meet each other. Anna and I were far from the first, far from special, but we did what the others didn't: last.

Perhaps as much as the fantasy of a workplace romance, it's a lasting workplace friendship that has my imagination captured. Lancaster and Collin Davison have been coworkers and friends for over twenty years. *We still hang out outside the show*, Lancaster tells food journalist Terrence Doyle in a 2019 interview. When she thinks about spending her workdays with such a long-standing friend, she says, *I feel really damn lucky. I keep waiting for someone to pull the rug out. Is this really happening?*

Night after night, I stand at the counter watching these dear friends teach viewers to make hearty, white-American standards as well as the occasional dish from elsewhere on earth. I consider the stability of that work. It feels like only days ago I was thinking about working in my shared office in an oncology clinic for the rest of my life, scrolling through the retirement benefits information, choosing who among my colleagues could be my lifelong work buddy.

Doyle wants to know what keeps *America's Test Kitchen* fresh.

I think each year we're looking to explore the evolution of what Americans think home cooking is.

It was only when Anna left campus and moved into a one-bedroom apartment in the city, a twenty-minute train ride away, that I realized she could not prepare food at all, had no sense of how to shop, how to plan, how to prepare a simple meal. She was five inches taller than me and had a personality larger than anyone else's. But being in a kitchen made her act anxious and unsure, so unlike the person I knew her to be.

I drove her to Trader Joe's downtown, watched her touch meals in packets and pouches, ready-made items on shelves and in freezers: chana masala, bean burrito. I bought chocolate-covered stuff to bring home to her sad, lonely, empty apartment. In IKEA, I named the items I put in the cart: saucepan, colander, box grater. Anna was a New Yorker and did not yet drive, so we put the thick blue plastic bags into the back of my Honda. Before this, we weren't required to be consumers, not in this way. We had bought each other small gifts, ice cream cones. We didn't accompany each other to buy our shampoo or our deodorant. We only saw the other spend fun money. Sometimes I bought her a cup of coffee or a bagel, with money I made at my campus jobs. As I watched her consider plates and mugs, I was jealous that she was done with school. I didn't want to read long history books anymore, didn't want to write my thesis. The idea of filling a completely empty apartment with my very own things thrilled me, but then, I had grown up with money and Anna had not.

In her abominably tiny, and yet sparsely filled and decorated, kitchen, I tried to show her how to make garlic spaghetti: slice the cloves as thin as you can with your new knife, heat oil gently in your new pan, cook pasta in your new pot, in heavily salted water. Anna had purchased two deep teal bowls, and we used two of the set's four forks to eat pasta at the little wooden table I had stained for her. A few weeks later, she called me in my dorm room. I was probably sitting on the floor, legs splayed out wide in front of me, book open between them. Anna reported that she had tried to make the pasta. It was so bad, she'd thrown it away. *And you know me*, she said. *I'll eat anything.*

Julia Collin Davison is making murgh makhani. Years after it was posted, I am cooking along. She isn't in the studio. She's at her home, like her actual house. At least, that's what I think it is. Each chef from *America's Test Kitchen* now cooks in a separate, spotlessly clean but not impeccably neat kitchen. I like watching her, and I make and like the recipe, but something is certainly lost when she's cooking by herself. She speaks of family, but they are not on the screen, and there is no evidence of children anywhere in the frame. I want to see them. I am angry they are not there. When I serve the dish to my kids, there is a ripple in my resolve, in my faith that I will make it through these months and years of working and parenting through a pandemic. I am thinking about how I am always cooking for children who are right in front of me, asking to put batteries in the remote, getting in my way as they fill their water bottles, asking when it will be ready. It enrages me that I can never get rid of them. What kind of parent am I? We didn't have even one of the kids accidentally. We had to go *way* out of our way, for each, and they didn't ask us to do any of that. It's not fair to them to want so much space from them, not fair that the things I seem to say most to them now are *Go Somewhere Else* and *Go Find Something To Do*, it's not fair that I'm jealous Anna leaves the house to go work at hospitals surging with the virus, it's not fair that other people in houses and apartments smaller and more cramped than mine can't afford the food I am stirring and stirring and stirring with vigorous rage. But reading the novel in which the mother gets in the car and drives away from her family in the night does not help, and reading the essay in which the poet cannot stop crying does not help, and reading the book about how class disparities affect the ways parents feed their children does not help. And even if I like making dinner tonight, when I am broiling chicken that Julia Collin Davison taught me to marinate in salted yogurt, the rage is there, just under the surface, waiting for me tomorrow.

I am thinking about how I'm learning to make dishes with ginger and garam masala and coriander from a white woman from Rochester, New York, whose early adulthood took her around the state, to college in Albany and culinary school in Hyde Park. Of course, the dish she's making, more commonly known as butter chicken, has been spun and spun and spun, spun off into chicken tikka masala and probably a million other Instagram-worthy things, you know the type, Indian-inspired tacos and wraps and pizzas, and what is authentic even, but still, the women I watch after work and while I cook dinner and at night when Anna is at the hospital are overwhelmingly, aggressively, white. I like to think I have an expansive imagination, that dinner is one of the places you could see it in action, but the truth is, I'm looking again and again into something like a mirror.

In a video from 2013, Bridget Lancaster teaches the viewer how to chop an onion. I love the way she says the word *onion*, like there's a *g* in it, *ongion*. She's from Cross Lanes, West Virginia, a few hours east of where Stella Parks was raised in Versailles, Kentucky.

In this painstaking, 4:24 video, we're instructed on all the different cuts we would need to make to achieve a decent dice. Watching this video, it's fully cemented that I'm not only looking for something to cook, I'm also just watching people do simple things, and they're talking to me while they do them. It's a comfort watch, no different from how other people watch true crime or the same sitcom over and over from start to finish. Maybe it's even more debased than that, like videos of people whispering, the kind you might use to fall asleep. I am trying to place myself in a state that is not on the plane of reality. The video is predictable. The onion is large and white, thick-skinned. I know how to dice an onion, have for a very long time. In Lancaster's capable hands, anyone could, after watching this. She looks young here, in her cobalt *America's Test Kitchen* coat and her blond ponytail. Anna and I are aging rapidly in these months. There are deep and fine lines sprouting new crease networks next to my eyes, and she's quickly going gray, especially on the left side of her head. People have been saying I look young my entire adult life, and it's finally not true anymore.

Lancaster has two children. When asked on KLCS whether she learned anything during the early pandemic, she noted the degree to which her world shrank around her husband and her sons. Her family is still in the South. *We found ourselves in a highly populated desert island*, she says, *because you just see people everywhere, you could see people walking around but you are on your own.*

Lancaster says, *Somebody once said to me, "Covid was the great accelerator," that anything that was going to happen in the next five years happened quickly.*

America's Test Kitchen is known, above all, for the rigors of its testing. Sometimes Bridget or Julia or one of the other cooks will tell their audience how many times they attempted a recipe before they decided on the version that works well enough to be called the best. For their Best Ground Beef Chili recipe, the *ATK* team perfected what Collin Davison calls *the Rodney Dangerfield of the chili world*. The team *tore the recipe apart at the seams* to gift me an elaborate many-step recipe that involves making one's own chili powder in the food processor, mixing ground beef with a baking soda slurry so that it cooks to a better texture, and grinding up tortilla chips into the mixture. When I finish watching, I have the same thought as YouTube viewer @garrett6064: *Sooo . . . the only thing I've been doing correctly is using beef. Time to up my chili game.* And it's amazing, but I can't help thinking about all the labor that went into figuring it out. That slow time. The payoff could be great, though, I think, watching Julia and Bridget eat large bowls of long-simmered chili.

Once I finished college, Anna and I churned through life stages: moves, jobs, kid after kid. It was like we couldn't stop, like we were some sort of millennial extremophiles, living our lives on hard mode for no reason. It was in the year everything shut down that we had finally vowed to stop changing our lives.

Claire

Claire Saffitz teaches her brother-in-law to make croquembouche. *He is quite the novice when it comes to baking*, Saffitz says in one of the video's opening shots.

I know I'm going to have a croquembouche at the end, Saffitz says. *We'll see what Nick ends up with.*

Nick, the novice in question, attends to Saffitz virtually. She has placed her laptop, which is worn and dusted with a bit of flour, atop an enormous hardcover book. Saffitz records in her home kitchen, which is modestly sized but larger than nearly every New York City kitchen I've seen. I love it more than any other food celebrity kitchen because of how real it feels, how true to my own life. The cabinets aren't nice and the appliances look old. There's a huge stack of cat food cans in one corner, and unlike many creators' kitchens, in which surfaces are bare but for what's needed for the recipe at hand, this one has everything out: tools overflowing from containers—tongs, ladles, spatulas—ingredients labeled with pieces of painter's tape, and in the corner, an ancient-looking toaster oven sits stacked on a microwave. As the twenty-four-minute video progresses, stuff accumulates in the sink and on the small drying rack beside it. If a dough rests for a day, you get to see a day's worth of life accumulate through the video's shots.

Croquembouche is a comically difficult dessert, a tower of profiteroles glued together with caramel and blanketed in spun sugar. Saffitz is confident she can make it in its entirety in four hours.

Nick *has huge Jack Black energy*, someone writes in the video's comments. He wears a long beard and a baseball cap. He cooks in a nicely renovated kitchen that's darker and less chaotic than Saffitz's. He has thick plastic glasses and a warm, goofy smile he lets loose whenever he accomplishes even a small step on his journey to make Saffitz's most difficult published dessert.

With Saffitz, I've found a chef whose video releases I follow religiously, instead of watching an archived back catalog. It's spring 2021 and my children are just returning to in-person schooling, after a full year at home. Claire Saffitz releases one video per week, and I watch them as I wait for my life to change.

Some are quitting their jobs. Others are just quiet quitting, doing the bare minimum, saving themselves from getting so emotionally wrapped up in their labor. Why should we commute to jobs that take place on screens? What do all these meetings even accomplish? People are changing careers and genders. Some are drinking more than usual and some are buying roller skates that look like the ones they used as kids. Anna and I watch with a sort of sick mixture of dread and glee as some people we know, now that they are stuck at home, adopt pets with intensive needs, especially puppies who require lots of walks, all that running around. *That puppy is going to be ruling their house*, I say, my face twisting into a cruel smile as I turn my phone screen toward my wife, knowing that the animal is not in danger but that my friend is. You would not believe how the dog park has exploded in popularity. It only took a few months of isolation before people our age and class began living this way, throwing out parts of their old lives, believing the one they're starting is the one that will stick. If we're going to be afraid to die so viscerally, we better live. Friends move out of New York and San Francisco. Why live in this damn city if I can work in my underwear, wherever my living room is? People are fleeing expensive places, gentrifying far-flung towns with their hybrid cars and their fussy tastes in coffee and beer. I flirt with Zillow, also, with a big escape. People like me, people who are conservative not in a political sense but in a personal comportment sense, we are in the kitchen. Yeast and flour are gone and everyone is learning to do new things. I've always liked to bake, but I've never been great at it, only passable, and in this time of learning I want to grow too. I used to go to the gym, I used to expend much of my selfish energy in the squat rack, but the gym is closed and I'm closed off in the kitchen. I used to dream of a better world, and now I am dreaming of projects, of loaves of bread, of layer cakes, of laminated pastries.

This is when I start watching Claire Saffitz. In early 2021, she breaks away from Bon Appétit and starts a YouTube channel of her own, *Claire Saffitz x Dessert Person*. Saffitz makes a layered carrot cake studded with pecans, sticky buns coated in a thick layer of walnut topping, coffee cake that actually tastes like coffee. In the earliest video—the focaccia one—she dresses casually, in a tie-dye T-shirt and dark-tan smock-style apron. Sometimes her hair is tied up loosely, but mostly it's down, shoulder-length and graying. She can't seem to keep her cat off the counter. She scolds him in the gentle way anyone with a cat would recognize, telling a creature who would never think to listen what to do.

Though in my head I have performed my own little queer readings of celebrity chefs, until now, I've been focused, above all, on the food, the workmanship of Sara Moulton and Julia Collin Davison and Bridget Lancaster in cooking videos primarily viewed like an aerobics class you move along to. They chop, you chop. They stir, you stir. Saffitz is different. I feel myself dipping into obsession, a kind of watching I can no longer participate in outside the home. She moves her hands a lot while she talks, but in the measured way a politician does, repeating gestures and movements. There's a cheeky smugness to the way she introduces hard recipes. *It's not that complicated*, she says at the beginning of her video for a three-layer carrot cake. *Not* ***that*** *complicated*, she repeats, with a sharp sarcastic edge. Though I can see so much of the kitchen and it feels so open, I try to see inside the refrigerator when she's retrieving something. I have access but I want more. What does she eat when she's off camera? What condiments and wines does she have stashed in the refrigerator door? Anna and I used to people watch, sitting outside a bar or a coffee shop. We would sit on a park bench while the kids ran around and quietly remark on the people around us: outfits, strollers, comportment. But people don't relate to each other this way anymore. And in some sense it's a relief. After all, didn't I look at others and filter them through my ideas of normal and not, as a reaction to a lifetime of being seen as living outside existing systems of categorization? If I had to name one reason for transition, it would be to make people stop looking at me. Alex Marzano-Lesnevich writes about a destabilization of the meaning of nonbinary existence in lockdown: when the "social" part of "social construct" ceases to exist, they ask, *How do I define my gender when I—accustomed to how visible my gender usually makes me—am no longer being watched?*

On the Zoom screens where I spend much of my days being watched in my own way, I am *Krys (Hospital School Program) (he/him)*. Given the human impulse to judge a face quickly, I haven't been misgendered in years. My own face is slim and bearded, and I wear large glasses and have a neat fade. Early on, it felt like something of a disguise, the changing features and hair, not a real me but just something different, better in some ways and worse in others. Some people say transition is when they really see themselves, but I'm not sure I recognized the start or end point, or any of the in-betweens.

Now that I'm not watched by anybody who isn't in my family, I like the way I look. Away from the gym, the subway, the hospital cafeteria, the meaning of my body shifts, becoming something that, more than ever, truly belongs to me. Beginning testosterone at twenty-eight was less an act of defiance than one of conformity. I didn't want to be confusing anymore. I was tired. I wanted to be read clearly as one thing or the other. It didn't matter to me what I felt, the nuances of it. Gender or whatever. What happened to me when a stranger saw me from across the schoolyard when we went to pick up our kids, that mattered much more than anybody understanding what was inside me. I wanted to be read as a bland white man. But now that I am, and now that nobody interacts with me in real life anymore, I feel I can decide to do anything I want with my body. Wear nothing, wear a dress, shave my face, keep a silly little mustache, stop trying to hide my body's shape, marked as it is by the life I've lived, as all bodies are. I am nearly five years on testosterone and I don't know if it'll be moving forward or backward or sideways, but I'm going to stop doing what I've been doing.

In watching Saffitz, I'm watching someone my own age strike out on her own, make something new, and that has me captivated.

When I find Saffitz's videos, I've just gone off testosterone. Like, I'm talking maybe two or three weeks. I didn't tell anyone I was going to do it, I just did it, quietly and privately. Maybe, I think, I'll make a big change, too, do a big thing, like the people I've been admiring and criticizing from afar.

If I'm being honest, I've never taken the medication correctly. Everyone acts like testosterone is such a big deal, but it's just something half of people make a lot of, and the big-dealness of it wore off years ago. On the internet, behind the avatars I've created with varying degrees of anonymity, I say what I wish someone had said to me, I tell people, *Try it! Don't wait till you're 100% sure!* Just as you can always go on, you can always stop. The prescription instructs me: *Inject 0.4 mLs (80 mg) into the muscle once a week for 150 days.* My first doctor told me I could take the hormone subcutaneously, so I inject it not into muscle but into the hairy, squishy part of me, an inch or so outside my belly button. But more than the delivery route, it's the once a week with which I fail to comply. Every few months, I decide I'm going to stick with my favorite day for the injections: Monday. Monday should be easy to remember! Mondays are for fresh starts, for pushing the kids out the door to be on their way to school, for opening my work email with the hope that this will be the week during which I never fall behind. Even the years I remember being terrible at school—fifth grade, eighth grade, all of high school—I've never dreaded a Monday. So on those weeks when I get to inject hormones on my favorite day, I wake up and I go right into the bathroom. I have a syringe and two needles, one big one for drawing the oil suspension up, one small one for injecting into my stomach fat. The week begins. But then, even if I remember for a few Mondays, inevitably I get to a Tuesday or Wednesday or Thursday and realize I missed my injection. Dammit, how does this happen every time!? Okay, I did it on Wednesday this week, so I'll do it on Wednesday again next week, I tell myself, and we all know what happens next.

That is how I've come to skip my first dose, due on a Sunday. I woke up knowing I was supposed to take the medicine, and I walked into the bathroom, opened the cabinet, fingered the vial's label. *Testosterone cypionate 200mg/mL.* Before T, I thought constantly about the sort of person I could be if I started. And how to explain what happened when I did? The truth is, nothing dramatic occurred. It's just that all the thinking got to stop. I no longer wondered, What if I did? I was just doing it. Was this what other people's lives were like?

Saffitz releases weekly videos on Thursdays, and they actually arrive on schedule. I get into the habit of watching her make a dessert while I make the kids dinner. Dinner, all of it, the mains, the sides, the one-pot wonders, the family-style make-your-own-taco-bowl spread, the dependable old standards even, it's all begun to feel like a slog.

What are the biggest challenges for you? asks an interviewer, in a video a comical number of people send to me.

Aretha Franklin scratches her head. *The biggest challenges for me . . . is trying to figure out what to cook for dinner. Nightly, you know, just night after night. What is it going to be tonight?*

The interviewer laughs and insists that Aretha Franklin can't possibly cook her own dinner. He's a white man. I'm sorry, I'm just going to say it, I assume that white men on television rarely do it all. Somebody somewhere is taking care of their bodies and their homes. There's a cutting rebuke in the way she looks at him when she responds.

Oh, please, she says. *I do my own washing, my own cooking, my own ironing, all of that.*

Her face is the face of work: cooking not as joyful or inspired, but rather as just another chore. There are some things in life you just have to do. She rolls her eyes at the interviewer the way I'd roll my eyes if someone asked if I put my own pillowcases on my own pillows or put my own socks on my own feet.

I am far from the only person who finds great joy in watching Claire Saffitz. Soon I have a series of text threads going about her recipes, and about not only her new YouTube channel but also her old videos, especially the ones where Bon Appétit editors had her try to make homemade versions of difficult confections, like Jelly Belly jelly beans and Butterfingers. I find those don't hit the right spot for me. I don't like to see her flustered or hustling. I'm drawn to her obsessively detailed recipes, her cookbooks with their photographs of the exact steps I find most difficult, her videos segmented to aid rewatching the trickiest portions.

When Julia Child, perhaps the ancestor of all the food creators I love, made it big, one of the things people liked about her was her candor and the realness, that she would go for half an hour without stopping, capturing both triumphs and errors. She once recalled making an onion soup so quickly that once she finished, she realized she still had eight minutes left and was forced to sit calmly and talk at the camera, running down the clock. That chaos, I find now, looking back at the spectacle of her, the momentous cultural event during which she was the eye of a great storm, is part of the point. So when I'm tempted to see Claire Saffitz as an heir to Julia—they both fell in love with cooking through French food, they both deviate from scripts about how women on television should look and behave, they both present some of the most impractical food I can think of as totally normal—I stop myself, because what is a YouTube video on your solo channel, started in the moment we were all trying to take the reins in whatever way our race and class and gender allowed, if not an act of utter control?

In 1996, Margaret Talbot wrote that *every age gets the household goddess it deserves.* According to Talbot, Martha Stewart is the "anti-Julia," *a corporate overachiever turned domestic superachiever.* Around the same time, when asked what was the "wackiest" thing that had happened to her while cooking, Stewart talked about choking on set while eating a nut, calling it "embarrassing and unacceptable." Scholar of food television Kathleen Collins writes, *If she can't forgive herself for an automatic physiological response, what will she think of us floundering in our kitchens daring to try one of her recipes?*

I like both types of makers, the real and the surreally perfect. But it's the latter, in these times of wobbly identity, that particularly call to me. I have experienced being alive mostly as a prolonged instance of failure: to be happy, to be productive, to make it through one single day without resenting the work of it. I like to see the creators succeed. Sure, I could drag myself through the steps of making a baguette, and if anything, no matter what, in the end my house would smell like bread. But it wouldn't look like something from a store, and I'm sure the texture would be off. It's calming, then, watching someone make something magical in an ordinary kitchen. In her Bon Appétit videos, Saffitz sometimes spectacularly failed. But in the shift to YouTube, one might argue, the creator has near-total control over what the viewer receives. The name of the creator drives engagement even more than the names of the past: Emeril, Rachael, Martha, Julia. This era involves a new set of expectations and the loss of others. Videos can be a minute or an hour, they can follow a strict script or be different every time. In this new landscape, Saffitz thrives. In each of her videos, she is cool, calm, collected, and, above all, controlled.

Control. The point of stopping T is to give me time to decide if I can handle having another baby. I'm thirty-four and have given birth once, when I was twenty-six. The push and pull of my agency is extreme: I could control taking the medication but not what it would do to me or how fast, and now I cannot control how I will feel as it leaves me, or how I will feel about that. And once I decide, I cannot control if I get pregnant quickly and easily, nor what it would be like, having a baby. An acquaintance who has delayed IVF in the early pandemic writes on social media that, in her view, it's irresponsible to have a baby now, when we don't know what the virus does to the pregnant person or to the baby, when healthcare systems are being pushed to near collapse. But Anna, I can see, is dizzy with delight that I'm even thinking about it. A baby is not for anyone or anything, it's a person with their own separate, sacred life. But to ignore the power it has in the lives of its parents is obviously silly. What is deciding to have a baby if not an exertion of belief in control, and of belief that our world will continue on?

Saffitz's brother-in-law Nick makes a croquembouche that hits some roadblocks, primarily pâte à choux that is too thin, which produces flat, uneven profiteroles. But he's positive and cooperative, and seems to be having a blast. He loosens Saffitz's control over her programming a bit. He's a nice addition.

On two sides of a digital divide, Saffitz and Nick roll out craquelin dough to place atop their choux buns and Nick says, *This looks like the* Millennium Falcon.

That's . . . Star *. . .* Trek? Saffitz says.

Oh my God, seriously? Nick says.

Wars! Saffitz quickly corrects herself.

Saffitz tells the viewer her sister wouldn't consent to a *Star Wars*–themed wedding, but she would allow Saffitz to make a *Star Wars*–themed cake, to satisfy Nick. You see a picture of the wedding cake, with a printed well wish: *May the Fourth Be with Nick and Jane 05.04.19.*

Deep into the process, Nick slowly dips pastry into caramel.

Are you regretting this whole project at this point, or no?

Absolutely not, Nick says.

Are you sick of it?

Uh, no, I feel like there's some fatigue.

Nick, under Claire's guidance, presses on.

In an interview with *The Spiel* about her bat mitzvah, Saffitz says, *I was a super high strung adolescent and very focused on achievement. I was type A, as I still am, and just high anxiety. But I coped with my anxiety back then the same way I do now: which is plan, prepare, and practice . . .*

I think my 13-year-old self would be shocked to find myself in a profession and in an area of my industry that is very public facing. I've never been a performer and I think it's easy to sort of see the videos and think, "Oh, you're performing." But it's really not. It's me being in an element where I'm really comfortable and having that captured on camera.

Anna has agreed to cook dinner tonight—chicken cutlet sandwiches, she says, with marinated roasted peppers I made over the weekend—and I am sitting upstairs at my desk staring at these two moments from the interview side by side. The smell of grease and meat wafts up toward me. If you do something after planning, preparing, and practicing, isn't what you do then, by nature, a performance?

Early in *Dessert Person*, Claire Saffitz articulates the purpose of her work: *Identifying as a dessert person isn't just about a love of baking and pastry and all things sweet. To me, it's an attitude; it's about embracing cooking and eating as fundamental sources of pleasure. This is a book about baking—most of it sweet, some of it savory—but, more broadly, it argues in favor of an approach to food that is celebratory, abundant, and at times a tad luxurious.*

After culinary school in Paris, Saffitz earned a master's degree in history, focusing on food history of the early modern period. So she knows the newness, relatively speaking, of the wide existence of the things she makes, cakes that use hundreds of grams of white flour, cups of powdered sugar, reliable dried yeast, semifreddo just because. For someone who is not incredibly wealthy to have these things on hand. It's not spoken, though. Creators like Saffitz do not talk about the things underneath their videos: race, class, gender, labor. When does she go to the store, and how much does she spend? How often does she buy takeout? Under what circumstances would she skip a meal because she just cannot bear to reenter the kitchen? Does her husband, Harris, a professional chef, cook dinner, or does she? These things are outside the scope of her project, which is to communicate directly with this figure she has identified, the *dessert person*. You want something sweet and she will teach you, step by painstaking step, to make it. There have always been, I'd imagine, people who craved sugar, who preferred fruit to nearly anything else on earth. Anna did not grow up in a house with any skilled bakers and yet she remembers the cherries and gooseberries from the Polish mountainsides of her youth. But nowhere is it spoken that to be a dessert person in the way she is, in the way I am, is a thoroughly modern way to be in the world.

Like Ina Garten and Julia Child before her, and like her contemporaries Alison Roman and Molly Baz, Claire Saffitz does not have children when I start watching her, start cooking her recipes. This is one of the things that strikes me as I watch these women, weighing my own imaginary second pregnancy. In the March 2020 Bon Appétit video "Pastry Chef Attempts to Make Gourmet Girl Scout Cookies," released the day after the pandemic shut down my children's school and all other schools in their district, the eighth largest in America, Saffitz declares, at the beginning of her attempt, *I haven't had Girl Scout Cookies in a very long time. I don't see any Girl Scouts around to, like, order cookies from!* There's a pause. From behind the camera, a crew member's (male) voice: *Do children like you?* Then a rip of crew laughter. *Yeah, I'm actually*—Claire laughs back, though through somewhat of a tight face—*I'm actually really good with kids*, she says. She shifts uncomfortably. *I just don't talk to them that much.*

Right around the same time, the poster vivahermione writes, on the subreddit r/childfree:

I secretly hope Claire Saffitz, my favorite celebrity baker, doesn't have kids because I look up to her so much. If she had kids, we wouldn't have that in common anymore.

I find myself envying friends who are pregnant, even strangers pushing strollers. Once I plant the idea of a fourth baby, Anna's work as a labor and delivery nurse takes on new urgency.

What would it change if Saffitz had a baby? I can't say that any more than I can say how it's changed my neighbors' lives to start gardening or to buy outdoor pizza ovens. There's no level of posting, of public persona creation, that would give me access to the real inside of someone else's life.

And I don't understand that Reddit poster, the one who feels they would lose their connection with Saffitz if she becomes a parent. I don't connect less with people who have no children. I'm as interested in people who make the same decisions I do as I am in thinking about the dream me who had done things another way, who had focused intently on the things they could do and could make in the years they had no children to care for, however many of those years there were.

In another video released around the same time, Saffitz joins fellow Bon Appétit cook Brad Leone's show *It's Alive*, which focuses on fermented foods, to make sourdough crêpes suzette. But while the intro is filming, Saffitz's attention wanders. As someone who came to her through her solo endeavors, it's surprising to see her behaving differently in the BA kitchen, surprising to see her distracted. She has, or portrays, at least, such intense focus. In these crowded set kitchens, the chefs of *America's Test Kitchen* ignore each other while the chefs of Bon Appétit have a put-upon-seeming convivial atmosphere, calling each other over to try a spoonful of something, or joking and jostling for attention, like an open office environment on a television show making fun of tech bros.

The thing that has distracted Saffitz is a coworker's baby, an adorable one, too, bald and blue-eyed and sweatered, maybe eight or nine months old, staring out the window with her father. The filming cuts and in the next shot, Saffitz is refilmed holding this baby, Thea, who is gnawing on an orange section, peel and pith and all, just shoving it into and out of her mouth, a wet stringy mess. Saffitz beams. *Did you know there are oranges in crêpes suzette?* she says to the baby. She is relaxed, looking at Thea as much as at the camera, bouncing the baby on her hips. My heart clenches, I don't mean that in the imagined, dramatic way you might think, I mean literally, food videos can affect my body and the way it works—there is a pulling sensation in my chest, a lurch of want and, in a way, of pain, wrapped up with all the joy my children have brought me. A moment before, Saffitz had been snottily telling Leone that *It's Alive* is the easiest show. She had been puffing out her chest, showing off, posturing. The way the baby softened her—it's as much proof that having a baby is a good way to spend your time and your life as it's proof that it isn't.

At work in the clinic, a friend, a psychologist, uses the fact that her patient cannot remember to inject a weekly medication as evidence that this patient is going to struggle.

My coworker seems like someone who, broadly, has her life more together than I have mine. But who's to say? We are all acting it out to some degree. Maybe my kids have clothes that are cheaper than her kids', and mine all share socks out of one bin because it's easier, just an incredible mound of worn black and grayed-white sock balls, and sometimes they have to bully me a bit to fold laundry because they're out of underwear, which is all threadbare or slack waisted, and they do it in a roundabout way, not saying, exactly, *Go fold laundry*, but rather, *I won't have any underwear tomorrow*, dot, dot, dot, and they don't have expensive hobbies, or hobbies that require driving more than a few minutes, and they go on deeply unfancy vacations, spending days car camping with their mother at cheap campsites, all in one big tent. We have all of what we need and most of what we want and little of what would be legible as nice to others. But if you ask my children what they eat on an average day, they'd likely name at least one impressive thing, some pastry or complicated dish. They've tried every fruit and vegetable I can think of. Are they all right, my kids? No one tells you really how you're supposed to know that, if you're doing enough, if you're doing the right thing. A part of me worried, when I started testosterone, that since transition was such a personal, such an inwardly focused thing to do, I would no longer have the time and space for my children. Was it an original thought or a thought that was placed in me externally, the word *selfish* applied to nearly anything a trans person does, in the ether of the anti-me internet? But doing an injection takes just a handful of minutes, if you're moving slowly. Close the bathroom door, unwrap the syringe, look in the mirror. Every week, you get to decide if you want to keep doing life the way you're doing it. And then you take the medication and it's over.

What no one really says about parenting is that you can't not do it, there is no way. There's no daily or weekly decision involved. It's like being at the bottom of a hill, and all the things the kids need are balls that must, by the nature of the universe, roll down. Being trans doesn't make me special, doesn't stop anything that needs to be done, the endless washing and feeding and caring.

I think about my coworker, someone I like and admire, who probably cannot understand how hard it is for me to remember to do this one thing for myself each week. *Weekly is hard*, I say, simply, but with a force and finality. Everyone, including me, rightfully avoids too much identification with our patients, because we don't have pediatric cancer, no matter what else we have going on. But there are things our patients struggle with that are our own little personal sinkholes. A task that doesn't flow downhill like a ball, one you need to go out of your way to remember. If I needed testosterone to survive, could I remember to take it?

There is a way trans people mark the time they've been taking hormones. It is an accumulation. One week on, one month on, one year on. Entire subgenres of the internet exist to document this linear movement from beginning to end, to the gender that is supposed to be final. When I was young, this was one of the things I spent much of my time online doing, watching others transition. And now, I'm not transitioning anymore. When am I off T? Is it the day I decide not to take it, is it when the hormone leaves my system entirely, is it when I get my period back? Or am I still on if I manage to maintain the gifts it's given me? The scripts for this are limited. What if I keep my beard, my jawline, my T-dick? When I decide to stop, I have been on for four years, eight months. When I tell Anna, I know she's looking for the emotional deterioration, for me to get grouchy, weepy, depressed even. She loves testosterone more than I do. What I'm waiting for is a sign. I don't know where it's going to come from, or what exactly it will be, but it's going to tell me whether or not I'm ready to try to have another baby.

For the first time, we get an Airbnb as a family. Before this, we have been in the thick of it, life with little kids, and we didn't take trips. I have joked that waiting to get my oil changed is my vacation, that a visit to the dentist is my idea of a trip. This one is my birthday gift to Anna, a cabin in Rowlesburg, West Virginia, and it's huge and remote and we can bring our dog and turn off the internet. We pack books and games. The second we're out of the car, the dog rolls in the mud. The only food store in town is closer to a dollar store than the supermarkets I'm used to, but it's okay, I can make dinner out of anything. I do hesitate about the way places like this, a neat little cabin done up for out-of-towners, may further extract from the most exploited region in the country, but we're not going to do anything except buy some groceries and hide away minding our own business. Anna has just recently started feeling confident she likely won't die from the virus—she was the first person I knew who got the vaccine, from her emergency room job, and I couldn't believe the flood of relief we felt the night she sat for the first dose—and though she still sees it, still sees people dying, still takes care of people who are gasping for air in the cramped hallways and rooms in which she works, Philadelphia never had refrigerated trucks to supplement the morgues, we never made international news, and this weekend is a minor celebration of being alive together.

It's late April and flurrying. We wear pajamas and layer jackets over them to go out into the acres and acres near the cabin. It's so thick that we don't make it far, just walk up and down some hills in the wet cold. We don't see or talk to anyone outside the family. We sit around a firepit, we play on the edge of a freezing river, we drink Lipton and eat flourless chocolate cake I bake in a springform pan I brought from home. The dog spends some more time lying in the mud. The kids play in the woods for hours with no supervision and we sit at the kitchen table reading. Think about how perfect it is, the life we have. Why would I want to fuck with this?

Claire Saffitz teaches me to make maple walnut sticky buns. Breakfast baking, Saffitz says, is her favorite category of baking. It's been years since I tried enriched dough, since I made bread at all. There was a phase, I remember only as I'm watching Saffitz toast walnuts and vowing to try this recipe for weekend brunch, when I made Melissa Clark's chocolate babka a handful of times, but I never felt confident I knew what I was feeling for as I kneaded the dough, what I was waiting for as I watched it rise. I brought two babkas to a welcome bonfire my first week of graduate school. *I care more about whether these turn out than I do about any short story*, I told Anna. I guess that means I knew the stakes could be high before all this, before the pandemic and this job and this decision. I turned the babkas out onto a plate and took them to my professor's house, where everyone was drinking and the sun was setting and the Michigan mosquitos were getting us; it didn't matter if the warm, chocolaty bread was perfect. I want to be like Claire Saffitz this time, want to be perfect. There's a moment of thrill when you turn over the pan, at least if you're a regular person like me. Saffitz doesn't look scared at all, scared the sticky filling won't come off the pan, scared she's wasted all these expensive ingredients on a failure. But I'm scared and I like it. I turn the buns out and they look just like they do in the video.

Cut to Nick, Claire's brother-in-law. His wife has made the same sticky buns and he is going to review them.

What do you taste? the person behind the camera asks.

Goodness, Nick says.

Claire Saffitz has over one million followers on YouTube, and a million on Instagram. Sales figures for cookbooks bumped in 2020, and she had one of the year's bestsellers. *The year might best be remembered*, Kim Severson wrote, *as the moment when project cooking became a national pastime*. Texts flood in from my coworkers when a patient for whom I've been advocating for months dies. It's not the first time it's happened, but it's the worst because the barriers to this patient attending school were so high, I spent months on the phone trying to make the experience better and I'm not sure I have anything to show for it. I can't handle the thought of screwing up a dessert, and now I have to deal with this? What, I wonder, do I have to show for any of it? Nobody swoops in to tell you you're doing a good job with your kids. I've never managed to stay at a workplace longer than two years. The feeling I'm doing nothing important overwhelms me and I start sending out applications and scheduling interviews. Anna is the same way, churning through the city's hospital systems, trying every type of nursing. We tell ourselves we have made good decisions, but we carry debt. We promise ourselves and each other that next year will be our turn to start settling, to focus on saving, to begin a life that might lead to something big we can be proud of.

Nick likes the sticky buns his wife has made, Claire's sticky bun recipe, but that doesn't satisfy Saffitz.

She remembers that her other sister made the sticky buns recently, for New Year's Day. *She never told me how they were,* Saffitz says, *which makes me think she did not like them. I will be following up about that.*

Do you think it'd be possible to call your sister real quick? Vinny, her cameraman, asks.

Saffitz cannot live with the thought that her recipe has not pleased the entire family. A million strangers are not enough. She says yes and picks up her phone.

How did Anna and I end up in a life that so narrowly focused on our own family's needs? A decade ago, this family felt to us like some radical act. Her father told her the day she came out that it would be wrong for her to have children. Protecting these fantasy children was his immediate reaction. It's not unique to him: having a child, having children, feels like it is still beyond the pale for a queer person to do, even though I know that there are others like me out there; even though I know some of them, they're not in my daily life. The only trans people who are in my daily life are my writing students, young adults who sign up for my classes in droves and who look to me as a person of authority and knowledge. I am in my thirties and I am a model of what a trans life can look like, surviving long enough to do the boring shit you used to think you were too cool to do. So when I was twenty-five and cradling my first baby on our beat-up couch in our run-down apartment, I felt radical. I was the first trans parent I knew. But over the years, our concept of what it means to lead a radical life, it's no longer about doing the things our parents thought we should not do. And it's certainly not this homonormativity, right? It can't be. In my young adulthood, just living to be an adult felt unimaginably hard, like I'd be living a life no one had told me was an option, and if I made it, then I'd have accomplished something.

Of course, a part of me thought Anna and I would do work that would change the world in a bigger way. After a few years of teaching, I would go back to school and become an education researcher. I wanted to be a part of devising policies that would bring best practices in including disabled children in classrooms with their nondisabled peers. My plan, my hope, was to start a career as a special education teacher as soon as I graduated. Special education teaching was a portable job, so I could go wherever I wanted to live in those early years. If Anna would have me, I'd gladly follow her, figuring, as I did, that she'd go on to a fancy school and a fancy life. She was so beautiful and so smart, so she had to! I would work a job and worry about a career later.

And Anna? She wasn't sure. She thought about applying to PhD programs in clinical psychology. She had a lot of ideas about how to transform behavioral health systems. She thought about applying to PhD programs in theater. She wrote beautiful plays. She could act and she could direct and, above all, she could write. But she knew people who left school and made experimental art, like the fringe stuff she studied in her classes, plays that took place in black box theaters and even non-theater spaces around the city, but when she heard the money these artists lived on, if you could call it living, she was shocked. Twelve thousand dollars a year, one friend half bragged, half confessed. Anna's father didn't flee communism for this! Art didn't make sense to either of us as a way to work. And so, partially to live and partially to have a way to stay close to me, since I was still in school, Anna took a low-level job in a behavioral science lab, one of a cadre of young, highly educated white people who coordinated research studies, first about schizophrenia, then about substance abuse disorders. After a few years of meager salaries and daily work she despised, she went to nursing school. After finishing, people kept asking when she'd go back for more school. Would she become a midwife? Another kind of nurse practitioner? Would she teach aspiring nurses? *I just want to go to work at the bedside and come home*, she'd say. Her work involves a kind of usefulness, I see now, that she feels right away, while she's doing it. In the years after college, I taught high school and then elementary school, but I never went on to become a researcher. At night, after wiping myself out teaching all day, I drove to a local university, one that was cheap and held very little prestige, and took classes with other exhausted teachers so that we could get our master's degrees and upgrade our teaching certifications. There was a separate pay scale for the people with these degrees, and that was how you got to a point where you could support a family with this work. Years into this, I went to writing school, and I felt guilty every time I thought about the union benefits and tidy salary schedule I'd given up to write about this queer domestic sphere. My space of resistance and containment. Sometimes one or both of us lamented about how the world was changing but we were not much a part of the change. I sought instant gratification then, too, in making Anna's favorite breakfasts and her favorite dinners and her favorite desserts. To socialize, we invite someone over for brunch. A coffee cake. Eggs in purgatory in a huge skillet. Our family life, our private sphere, became the place taking up most of what we had to give.

Claire Saffitz buys a house upstate. Of course she does. We are basically the same age—Saffitz is nine months older than I am—and so I am sure the dream of a something else has captured her too. At the upstate house, there are projects. There is a kitchen, not a beautiful kitchen, just larger than the one in her apartment, with lots of labeled bins and not a lot of care shown in its design, and it will need to become the kitchen shared by two professional chefs. There are plans for an outdoor oven and for a chicken coop.

The fourth baby will be my pandemic sourdough is an insane thought I have one night while falling asleep.

Unlike some of the other women I love to watch, Saffitz doesn't pretend she doesn't know what she knows. She's honest about things that are hard, things that took her a while to figure out, things that she learned to make in culinary school, but in the end, there's no humility in the product she's teaching you to make. She has moved through the long early adulthood I worry I'm stuck in, and she exudes confidence about what she's doing. *What do I know?* I catch myself saying, at work or at home, after a sentence I should have delivered more confidently. People seem to think I'm grown-up because I have children, but there's no test to make sure you're ready, it's just something you can do. Saffitz promises the final boss brownie, the final boss croissant. Every recipe, every video, is a successful pitch for the treat you might get if you follow every single step perfectly. I can tell when she presents the recipe at the beginning, showing the cast of ingredients, when she talks about how she arrived at each step, that there is such a precision and study involved in what she's done, that it has nothing to do with me, an amateur home baker.

The thing about developing a recipe for kouign-amann you believe a home baker could follow is that it requires an ability any great teacher has: to predict where your followers might go wrong, to be able to see inside them and get ahead of that.

When I watch other creators, envy seeps into my thoughts about them from every corner—I want their apartments, I want their pantries and refrigerators, I want their money, I want their lives—but I don't envy Claire Saffitz. I am just thankful I get to watch.

When, occasionally, I wonder about the hours and days I either use or lose reading cookbooks and, more than that, viewing cooking programs, I quickly realize it's right in front of me, what I'm turning away from, not just my own ultimately puny questions about my identity and my morality, but the bigness of all that could happen and that is happening to other people, at this moment and every other moment that will ever occur. The threat of death is everywhere, so of course I'm thinking about making things, brownies, pies, and a baby.

It's right there, in the first few sentences I read on the very first day of my job:

Prior to 1960, acute lymphoblastic leukemia (ALL) was almost invariably fatal. Fortunately, improvements in treatment have reduced the mortality rate to such an extent that ALL is now viewed as a chronic life-threatening illness (Brown & Madan-Swain, 1993). However, improved survival rates have not been achieved without neuropsychological sequelae.

Only a tiny number of people nationwide do the job I do at the hospital, which is a low-level, but specialized, job. What I'm saying is that there's no room for movement, either up or laterally. It's not even just the money, the fact that I will never make it to House Upstate Status, it's just knowing you can never do more with any given day. The most I can do is be the very best at sending the same emails I'm already sending, or perform better in the next virtual school meeting than I did in the last. I'm losing faith in my ability to keep doing something in this steady, even manner. There are so many things about this job I don't care to talk about, but I like how Anna laughs when I describe the different ways I try to make schools do what a child's doctor or neuropsychologist says they need in order to be successful in school. She has never had a job that involved sending emails. Her work is done with the body far more than with the mind. The way I describe my job to Anna, I could be sending emails about anything. Despite the fact that my work badge says *Oncology*, cancer, to me, is, disturbingly, becoming something that takes place over email. *Bumping this up in your inbox with the semester starting so soon! Thanks in advance for your help! Let me know what I can do to make sure this plan goes off without a hitch! Appreciate your partnership in solving this problem!* Only, of course, the emails are all about sick kids. It's easier to laugh about my silly, faux-slapstick menacing email performances than to talk about things like highlighting, in every introductory message I send, the words ***life-threatening illness***, hoping it will get me somewhere. Every job involves being someone you're not for all or part of the day, but there's got to be some way to make a living where you get to share more of the person you are, right?

Four was what we agreed was the goal. Four children. This, we agreed, was when your family started deserving the title *big*. What is the meaning, exactly, of an intention you set years before you know anything? When I was in college, I babysat for a family with four children, each a year to a year and a half younger than the last. Sometimes Anna came along. This was perfect, we decided. Six, what I'd grown up with, was too many children, but three, what she'd grown up with, was not enough.

But then there's the reality. You have one kid and it wrecks your marriage a little, you have a second and it wrecks your marriage more, you have a third and maybe we can't actually keep doing this? I mean, we can, but we shouldn't, because who wants to live with someone you hate? The way resentment can fester over the littlest things, a diaper someone didn't throw in a pail, a diaper bag left behind on a hook in the living room in someone's delirium. That time, the period when your baby is new, it's too hard to keep doing. So we do other things, only really it's more of the same things we've signed up for by way of the choices we made: making breakfast, making lunch, making dinner, doing laundry, drop-off, pickup, Friday Disney movie, the electricity bill, online grocery shopping, in-person grocery shopping, a family Trouble! tournament, online shopping for yet another pair of new sneakers for everyone, school uniform shopping, *Mario Party* on Saturday morning.

On its face, Claire Saffitz's larger project seems to be a sort of task analysis, breaking down complicated recipes into steps that are so clear and incremental that even novices can attempt them. Like how, I learned in teacher school, the key to giving access to everyone was in identifying all the fault lines in a complex task, whether it was long division or opening a locker. Claire Saffitz is doing this for the layer cake. A demystification, democratization, of baking. But viewed another way, she is teaching us to make things—sourdough loaves, cannoli shells, croissants—that, typically, we've come to see as store-bought items. It could be said that I didn't think I should try to make cannoli until I saw her do it. In that way, work like hers is part of a larger cultural trend, especially in American heterosexual internet culture, that of sharp increases in our expectation of performance in the kitchen and in the home in general.

What is someone making food content giving to the world? On the subreddit r/clairesaffitz, which has just under four thousand members, users post photographs of desserts. It's extremely wholesome, with commenters sharing their own experiences with the cake or halvah or tart that's been posted. One recent post does not contain a photograph of a dessert. Instead, the photograph is of the pages from Saffitz's *Dessert Person* in which she lays out the time and difficulty level of each of the book's 105 recipes. The poster writes:

I was gifted my copy of dessert person by a friend for my birthday in Jan 2020, and I really didn't start baking with it until 2021. I started crossing off recipes that I'd finished on the recipe matrix. The process of marking each recipe complete was so oddly satisfying that I decided to bake every recipe in the book. It's taken me about 2.5 years to get through 37 recipes (including many foundational recipes) and I will not stop until I have completed the matrix

There's something comforting to me about this, this person's ability to take something small, like a cookie recipe, and turn it into a yearslong quest. It represents a hope in the future, that it will keep happening, that there are many joyful things in store.

How to describe the relief of having Anna return home in one piece after every shift? Anna does not catch the virus, does not bring it into our house. She stands by the front door, putting her hand on it to support herself, as she strips off her scrub pants and her scrub top. She hands them to me. In these moments, instead of seeming sexy, her half-naked body strikes me as unbelievably vulnerable. Her stark-white skin, the moles I know so well. I wash the clothes again, fold them just after the dryer is done, so they won't wrinkle. It's all that I can do. The children know they are not to hug Anna right after she gets off work. Will they ever unlearn this distance?

In the backyard, Anna and I turn on the string of lights and sit in the fresh air, even when it gets cold. We consider buying a heat lamp, but instead just become people who have opinions about tea, purchasing samples in little metal tins. We sit outside under blankets, holding steaming mugs. On Mondays, I feed the kids something quick right after work and, late into the night, make Anna simple pastas while she sits at the counter.

In the moments before Saffitz removes the maple walnut sticky buns from the oven, she receives a call from her cat's vet. She takes the call. *You guys*, she says. *He's still not eating, and they might have to put a feeding tube in. My poor kitty.*

All right, I'm now so depressed, I'm going to pull these maple buns out of the oven.

And then there they are: a dozen perfectly even buns, cradled in a mourning woman's hand.

The slogan on a T-shirt Anna used to wear, when she studied psychology as an undergraduate: *Love is the misattribution of arousal in the presence of an appropriate other.*

Anna and I are firing on all cylinders in these months, feeling existential dread about our safety, about our parents' safety, complicated as that is, about our friends who take risks we wouldn't. We fret over every decision we make. What will we feel if we get mortally ill inside a gas station, inside a doughnut shop? But something else happens too: we love like we haven't in years. We are lonely and we turn to the only thing we have, the person who's been right in front of us all along. Suddenly, touching her feels electric, like when we first met and would make out in the basement of the campus library, by the big gray shelves of government documents that surely no one needed to look at, not at this hour. We are hiding from the kids, kissing in the kitchen. We are smoking secret cigarettes in the backyard and holding the other's free hand. We have outdoor dinner dates there, eating homemade hummus and pita, little cups full of nuts. Some nights we sit on the couch together, me with a beer, her with a cider. Hours tick by even though we both have to work tomorrow. We are staying up too late and we're not even watching reality TV, we're just talking.

I am in my midthirties and I am in love. And I've made my decision. One of those late nights on the couch, I say it: *I want to have another baby.*

I've been pregnant before, but that was before transition, and I don't know what to expect. I am giving it time, seeing if I feel good, taking a few months to myself before I go ahead and try to get pregnant. I keep doing the things I was doing before, with slight variations: each day I am logging on to work, but we're making plans for me to return to the office part-time once it's summer again. The kids are still online for part of the week, but they've been going to school in-person a few days a week again. Things that didn't feel possible weeks and months ago are rearranging themselves into a new future.

In our neighborhood, the men have vague artistic careers while the women, some of whom are also artists of some sort or another, work as professors or art teachers or in offices at universities or nonprofits. In this group, the flipped gender dynamics in my own home are nothing special. Being a feminine man is deeply unremarkable. We gather on the playground in our denim shirts, holding our coffee cups and bags of snacks for the kids. I say *men* and *women* because hardly anyone is queer, at least not in any way that leads to something other than one man / one woman / one-to-two-kid family units.

Claire Saffitz's brother-in-law looks like any of the middle-aged white dads I know. Nick pleases Claire with his pastry cream, but when he shows her his pâte à choux across the digital divide, she frowns, then quickly fixes her face, telling him it will be okay. In the end, when he tries to arrange his flat buns into a gleaming tower of pastry, they come together in something of a squat globe.

Hers is perfect, rising off the counter majestically, coated in spun caramel.

Nick pops one choux bun after the other into his mouth, shrugging Claire off when she asks if this felt like a waste of his time. He acts thoroughly like someone who isn't being watched.

Okay, I just have one question, she says. *Was it worth it to spend the last seven hours doing this?*

Was it worth it? I mean, trying new things, and having something to show for it?

Claire is genuinely surprised.

What a great attitude, I love that attitude, and I couldn't agree more.

What would it mean to spend time well, and what would it mean to waste time? Are the years I am spending with my young children being spent in the best way, or in a way that occludes my chance to be a public person, a person who does things that better the world? The thing is that I'm really asking, because I don't know how I'm supposed to spend the time I have. Raised in a housing complex in Warsaw before the wall fell, Anna leans into the improbability of the life we have: the queer family, the children we've made with a man we only met because of the lengthy series of choices we made. Now that this alchemy has led to the so-muchness of our lives, we should enjoy it. She doesn't want more than family and a few friends. Her favorite year was the one we were most relaxed, when we had chill jobs and just enough money to cover the basics and spent many evenings outside in lawn chairs smoking when the kids went to bed. *I never want anyone to ask me what's next*, she said one night, looking out onto the dark, empty street in the small town where we spent three years. We had both been conditioned to strive. In a photo from that year, taken by our oldest, we pose on a wooden bridge in front of a small inland lake and its shoreline, dotted with trees. Hiking is one of the only ways I feel good doing something that accomplishes nothing. I love the different ways the kids approach it, one holding our hands talking, one running and jumping, one trailing behind. Anna wraps her arms around me and we press our heads together. But in the photo, we're blurry as fuck. You can't see our facial expressions well, though if you know us, you can intuit that we're smiling. In front of us, a giant head sticks up from the bottom of the frame, cutting off half our bodies. Our second son is in perfect focus, his hair in a tiny ponytail on the top of his head, his tongue out wide, his eyes squeezed in twin devilish eye-grins. *Romance after children*, my caption reads.

Unlike the changes that come with going on testosterone, which occurred dramatically in a way anyone in my life could see—the new, rippling muscles, the squarer face, the hair—the changes going off are slow and subtle, visible only to someone looking ever so closely at my face. Although being on the medication stopped defining my life long ago, I now worry I identify mainly as someone not on it. I am waiting to move in reverse. For the first month or two, I look and feel the same, and then I change little by little. I take stock every few weeks. I am thicker in the hips and my breasts are fuller again. And for all the papers I was handed warning me in bolded letters that genital changes were permanent, I'm back to the way I was before, smaller, softer and healthier on the inside. We still fuck, but we don't joke about my big dick anymore. I become a bored, unenthusiastic top, and I try to pretend that's not the case. We don't joke about how I get to be a boy for one more week after I take the injection. We don't tell any trans jokes anymore. I get a period.

In the work bathroom, I cover the evidence with an obscene amount of toilet paper. I cry when I'm sad. I become frustrated easily. But I notice the change most of all around my mouth, in the way my cheeks are rounder again, the way my beard thins and softens, the lightening of the hair there. It never occurred to me how much I liked those scraggly little red hairs before they started disappearing. When someone takes a picture of me, sometimes it's like I don't have a beard at all, like I'm yet again somebody else.

On the hour-long commute to the office, in my hard pants and my mask, I have, for the first time in over a year, the space to intellectualize my domestic labor. For example, if everything about society were different, or if I had made different choices at every turn in my adult life, I would not need to make dinner as much, maybe even never at all. I could split the work with another family, or society could offer another place to go get fed. If there were a place I could take my family to eat that was not my home and not a restaurant, I would.

In her essay "I Dream of Canteens," Rebecca May Johnson reflects on British Restaurants, thousands of publicly funded canteens that served mass communal meals during and after World War II across Britain, ultimately feeding over half a million people each day. In the immediate aftermath of the destruction of much of the nation, this public service seemed reasonable to everyone, but once proposed as a possible long-term solution to hunger, conservatives turned away from them. The closest contemporary parallel to the British Restaurants Johnson can think of is the café at IKEA, a place you go when you're tired of shopping and walking and pay a few bucks for a hot meal in a clean place where you can stay a while. The food is a benefit but not the only one: *The levels of pleasure derived from eating a meal or drinking a drink without the anxieties of restricted time and space and money can be great indeed*, Johnson writes.

I love how Johnson flips IKEA, this place of domestic striving, into a landscape of communal ecstasy and relief. In a world with canteens, would I love cooking more? Can someone just tell me what to make tonight? Somebody please entertain my children for a minute so I can get this chicken into the pan? Is there a world in which I can continue to pay the incredible grocery markup for delivery and not feel guilty and not bankrupt my family? Is there a world in which I have the time and patience to teach anyone else in this family to cook? I want to take them to a canteen but there is no canteen, only my kitchen, my table, my my my.

Now that I am back at the office, I try to reclaim what made me love working in the clinic in the first place: pure, unclouded purpose. I want to be like Claire Saffitz developing the hundred-plus recipes that make up *Dessert Person.*

The walk to the subway is over half a mile, and the walk from subway to hospital is over half a mile, and by the time I get inside the gleaming tower of offices and change my shirt in the first-floor bathroom and head to the elevator, I'm tired out and ready to sit at a desk. But even when I sit face-to-face with a patient in their exam room, their parent explaining to me what happens in math class, and what sorts of difficulty they are having learning to add and subtract, the purpose never fully settles. I make the faces of someone who is attentive and sympathetic, and I continue to perform the actions well—explaining special education law, attending the school meetings, and making nice enough with teachers and counselors to get things done—but I've been changed by all this time being just an avatar, a voice on a telephone, a collection of words in an inbox. I feel unreal, useless in some fundamental way. On my way home, my legs cry out from all the standing and the walking to and from and around the clinic, and I consider that when I get home, around six, I'll have to prepare dinner quickly, as if I'm on a cooking show. My tired hands will ferociously smash garlic cloves, turn my can opener, shake drained pasta dry.

The more days I spend at the office, the more engrossed I am in work on the days that I'm home, the less pleasure cooking offers me. So focused on the transition back to work and on the way my body is or isn't changing, I haven't had the presence of mind to make a dessert in weeks. When the kids are done eating, I toss chocolates at them from across the room, like they're captive seals and I am pitching dead fish in their direction.

If dessert is, perhaps by definition, something one wants but does not need, why do I feel like that definition is not true for me? Sure, there are nights I sit down proud about what I made for dinner, but it's the desserts that take me into some other realm, a plane of higher functioning I can't touch otherwise. It is Claire Saffitz, above all, who has taken me there. Just before my birthday, I've been off testosterone for six months and I've made my peace with how I feel, and I'm ready to try to have a baby. My favorite thing about my birthdays ever since I started testosterone is that I can see the future now, I can grow old in this imperfect world of daily labor. The work isn't just to get to bedtime that day, it's a building block atop which I build days and weeks and years that will hold, along with everything else good and bad, me. This is why, though I've complained here and elsewhere about the labor of feeding us—the shopping, the dicing, the stirring, the baking—and I often long for a solution, for other ways of living together with partners, with community who will take some of the work away from me, who will give me new work to benefit those outside my family, I don't think about any of that on my birthdays. It's June, the best month, the cleaving of spring to and from summer, the fruit at the market, school letting out, sun everywhere. I have come to treasure as my one sacred ritual making my own birthday cake, exerting that control, dreaming my own dream and then bringing it to life. All that butter and flour and time, my time, stretching out before me.

Deb

Hannah Goldfield writes: *Deb, as her friends, family, and most loyal fans call her, deserves to be mentioned in the same breath as Martha and Ina, but she is not selling a fantasy of domestic bliss. She simply wants to eat well, and to show you how to do the same.*

I am home alone in the middle of my workday when the nurse practitioner calls me. Anna is out with the kids running errands, and I am standing in the living room taking a break, doing the thing I do every day: running through a mental checklist of what we have in the fridge, what I could use to pull together a dinner. The conversation is brief, and only after it's over do I begin to understand what has happened. She does not use any of the words that would communicate my degree of infertility to me. She says the names of hormones and then she says numbers, and then she says something I can barely process about how we need to begin treatment immediately. Whatever is wrong with me is only getting worse. On the corner of the envelope where I take notes there are letters and numbers, but I don't know what anything stands for. FSH, AMH, one far too high, the other far too low. We hadn't had trouble, making the other children. They were born out of hospital, at a birth center, dimly lit and calm, serene and sacred nights. We believed the possibility of the four children was simply frozen in a cryobank as we fell into and through our thirties, into and out of jobs and apartments and periods when we loved each other fiercely and others when we tired of the things the other wanted and cared about. Sometimes, for months, I did not focus on the stories Anna told me about work and her friends and the books she was reading because I could not pay attention, lost as I was in whatever I was lost in. That voice again: *Listen, pay attention, stop moving, stop moving*. By the time she'd reach the end of her sentence, I knew from her eyes that I'd missed most of what she'd said. It was the same with the kids, my inattention chewing up the middles of so many of their questions and stories.

Anna and I joke that this imagined fourth baby is the only one we both want, and even though she is only a dream, only a wish, she is a foundation on which we are building some future domestic bliss. It's a phrase we've used before, but only sardonically. *Domestic bliss*, we'd say to each other, when we were trying to parent while sick, lying half dead on the couch handing our children our phones, ice pops, even our wallets, so they could pull each card out and throw them all in a heap on the ground, anything that would make them let us rest, or when a child defaced a rental home with elaborate pen drawings on their bedroom walls, and not even pictures or words, just shocking, violent scribbles. But now, years after the last time, we have a vision of strollers and baby wraps and the most perfect stash of never-been-used cloth diapers, lined up in a row on one of the wheeling carts we used for virtual school, each child's roving desk. It's not just the stuff of babies, but also the baby herself, in our arms, in our kids' arms, and at the dinner table as she gets older. Her fingers, her hair. We could be, should be, six. Nobody deserves their dream, but ours feels so doable.

And I have my own private vision, too, that having another baby will feel different, better, than when I did it nearly a decade ago. Back then, before transition, I felt like I was watching myself. There was a vast gulf between me and the baby, even though he was inside me. This time, I'd be able to feel the import of what I was doing in real time, while I was doing it, in the right body, in the right gender, at the right time. The baby and I would be a team—I'd really be there for her, with her.

What does Hannah Goldfield mean, in saying that Deb Perelman, author of the food blog *Smitten Kitchen*, my culinary North Star, isn't selling domestic bliss? She feels so real to me, a sense that has only increased in the fifteen years I've followed her every recipe, her every cookbook. She's selling bliss of a sort, the bliss that I want right now—projecting satisfaction with the life you have. She has two young children and a New York apartment and a husband, and a dependable recipe for anything you'd conceivably want to cook. She's selling that, coming through with the right pasta in a pinch. What she's not selling is Ina Garten's gay-adjacent glamour or Martha Stewart's perfection.

But in the freefall of 2021, a year in which I stop taking testosterone, decide to have a baby, find out I'm infertile, and begin to weigh which treatments to agree to, if I decide to go through this at all, I turn again and again, as I have in every difficult moment of my adult life, to Deb Perelman's recipes, to the way, as Goldfield points out in her interview with Perelman, that she seems to have solved with a cake or salad every conceivable life problem that will come one's way. Will she be able to help me with this one?

It was the pictures of the food more than anything else that captured my young adult attention and endeared me to Perelman. In the blog's first post, "freedom, ringing," dated June 30, 2006, there is no recipe, only a close-up photograph of cherries, glistening with droplets of water, on a white background. Foregrounded are two cherries leaning against each other, their stems an otherworldly, grassy green.

In the early days, Perelman says now, she barely tested the recipes she posted, just curated things she found from a wide variety of sources, and shared how she tweaked them. She read, and ate, widely. Her practice has become professionalized over the years, and she now will try recipes again and again with many variations, but the basics of the blog have remained the same. The aesthetic has been with me so long, longer than most of my friendships.

Perelman isn't losing focus, she says. She still loves what she does, testing recipes, sharing them.

This applies to nothing else in my life—not sweaters or dresses, wall art, or even kitchen scales—

Perelman taught me to make lasagna with homemade noodles, grandma pizza, the smoothest hummus, chana masala, mushroom bourguignon. If I didn't know how to do those things, I wouldn't be me. The things that I do, as I age, are becoming more important to me than the things that I am. And it wouldn't be exaggerating it to say that, maybe as much as my mother, Perelman taught me to cook. With my laptop propped open on the countertops in the six homes I have shared with Anna since the beginning of the blog, I have followed along with Perelman's inviting, convivial, friend-like voice. She isn't someone I think of as belonging to the world of videos or podcasts. She exists for me primarily in text and image, someone I met through her increasingly professional-looking photography of her own mixing bowls, mixing spoons, dinner experiments, of her hands.

She's always been straightforward about the fact that she has kids and cooks for them. And that it's not always that great. When Goldfield asks her if she ever gets sick of cooking, she says, *Oh my God, all the time . . . I don't feel like cooking at least a couple days a week.* Maybe real domestic bliss is being able to be frank about what it is in your home that you most dread on any given day.

In September 2009, she shared a picture alongside a post titled "look what we baked!" In a close-up of her first child's head, you see a wonderful whorl of dark, downy baby hair, something you only understand if you've touched, really felt, a newborn's head.

Of course, we immediately tried to eat him. Because he has CINNAMON SWIRL hair.

Domestic bliss. Ask me before going off T what it was, and I would have said something other than what I would say now: having four children. I wasn't unhappy before, but now I know that nothing other than this baby will make me happy. The clarity is startling, and I'm ashamed of how nakedly I want it. I have never been surer of anything, not marriage, not transition, not any place I've lived or job I've worked.

I drove to my dream college worrying I'd made a mistake, fought horribly with Anna the day before our wedding—she made me let her out of the car on the side of a suburban road, in a town whose name she didn't even know—and asked the doctor who first prescribed my testosterone if I could take the vial home and inject it there, foregoing the lesson on needle use, because how could I finally cross the threshold into totally sure with a medical professional watching?

I explain all this, in much fewer and much less dramatic words, to a friend I have not seen in a while. It's been just a few weeks since I found out I'm infertile. I need time away from home, so we sit outside a coffee shop near his apartment for hours. He has the kind of life a small part of me longs for, before the other 90 percent of me tells that voice to get real. He lives in a cool neighborhood, has an impressive job, sees friends, not just by running into them in sweats on the way to school, or gathering every iota of energy to leave his neighborhood once every few months. My friend doesn't have children, doesn't like them, he's confessed. There's something almost unspeakably messy to me about explaining to anyone why I want this baby, doesn't matter whether they have or want kids. I hate the gut feeling

I get that my world will always feel tilted if I don't get to do this thing that I want, that I have already done, that what I really want is four children: embarrassing, infuriating excess.

From July 2013's "Hot Fudge Sundae Cake": *I want you to know that I think making a hot fudge sundae cake with homemade chocolate and vanilla ice creams, homemade Oreo-like cookie crumbles, homemade hot fudge sauce, homemade whipped cream and then, I mean, of course storebought maraschino cherries (because come on), is absolute madness. There is no sane reason to do this.*

After the coffee date, the first time I tell someone the whole story, from beginning to end, I sit in the park and read an entire book from beginning to end. It's a park I don't go to often, pushed up as it is against the river bounding the city's west end. Kids play with dogs. Kids play with Frisbees. I am a parent, but not right now, not when I'm away from my kids, when I am alone in a park after confessing for the first time the lengths to which I'm willing to go to be one again. Is parenting something I am, or is it something I do?

The book is Kristen Radtke's *Seek You: A Journey Through American Loneliness*. Like Deb Perelman, Radtke lives in New York, the city where I was born and where I spent my early childhood. She grew up in a quiet Wisconsin town, and the sensory overload of the city unexpectedly triggers feelings of isolation. In one of the most affecting moments in the book, she reflects on how profoundly lonely you can feel in a crowded city, watching strangers get on with their days.

> *When I walk down a street at night and catch the corner of a bedroom beyond a window's curtain, or see a woman fumbling for her keys on her apartment's front stoop, I'm surprised by the longing I feel for the people I pass, and the homes I'll never be invited into—or, perhaps more accurately, for the lives I'll never live.*

Perelman started her blog during a time in her life when she felt she did not have enough. She majored in psychology and fine arts, she tells Ethan Frisch in an interview, *because I was extremely indecisive.*

When she began her food blog, Perelman was working as a staff writer for a tech magazine. But she started her working life as an art therapist at a nursing home, having earned a master's degree in art therapy immediately after undergrad. *I liked working with old people*, she tells Goldfield, *but I realized that I had absolutely chosen the wrong career path. It did not make me happy.*

I didn't know what else I was going to do with my life. Like, how do you get out of such a niche profession?

Blogging gave her permission to experiment, helped her work her way into food writing. She tells Frisch, *Back then, you did not need to have, like, a focus and, like, a social media strategy—social media didn't exist.*

Maybe that's the thing—not only was Perelman not selling domestic bliss, she wasn't selling anything. It was just this incredible free resource through which Perelman could share with me the butterscotch pudding popsicles that had transformed her day, across time and space, and I could take them and do the same. I, too, had a blog in some of my young adult years, where I chronicled Anna's first pregnancy and all my thoughts about having a new baby.

Only my friends read it, which was the hope. I didn't have a take, an angle, the blog just gave me an outlet when I came home from work. I was the first person I knew to have kids. I didn't have a vision of what it would be, I didn't imagine bliss, I just knew that I felt incomplete on my own and incomplete still with just one other person living in my home.

Playing in Shenandoah.

That is how I caption the post about our trip to the national park. We are on a getaway in the woods again. In my favorite photo, I can see all three of my children, the fastest and most agile, the wildest, far in the distance, a red speck; his sister in the middle, wearing a pink dress that almost blends in with the crushed brown trail; and directly in the middle of the frame, a son pointing a stick at the camera, looking caught off guard. Writing about this, I feel a stirring distance from the me who took the picture: these three people are perfect, always have been.

Anna and I have started leaving them home alone at night, started taking dim early-evening or even starlit walks through our neighborhood. You have the things you worry about that you have to move past. For me, the fears are strongest when they're awake and we run across the street or take the dog out without them. What if they try to cook, or slip in the shower? For her, it's what if there's a house fire and it's night, and they're asleep? Anna seems to think that if we're in motion, if we're walking, talking about the dream baby might be easier, and on one level she's not wrong. I am better in motion. But I realize that so much of the way I conduct myself in a decision-making conversation involves trying to manipulate the other person into telling me what to do. Infertility brings along with it decisions. How hard will you try, to what lengths will you go? Now, on top of the daily, hourly, minute-by-minute buzzing of decision-making, of having a job and a life and three children, there are big questions: Would I take fertility medications? Which ones? Would we switch to Anna carrying? Would we give up?

On the drive to Shenandoah, I try to weigh as objectively as I can my thankfulness for the three kids I have against what it would take to have another. They are in the back of the car fighting, then watching movies on devices. In our tentative planning conversations, we've talked about the age at which Anna thinks she could take a baby camping, the age at which we would book a cabin like this one and still have the experience resemble fun. We thought about what we would do once the kid was here, but not how hard we would try to have it happen. A few months ago, by the little creek in West Virginia, we ate *Smitten Kitchen*'s chicken and dumplings, or an approximation of it, whatever I could put together with what I found at the little store in town. These recipes are something I take with me wherever I go. To bring something with me across state lines, the steps I had learned making Deb Perelman's creamy soup, to remember the methods if not the exact proportions, cooking, as I was, without internet, felt magical.

From her recipe: *Now, I'm not of the belief that chicken soup can cure a world of problems—I don't think it's going to fix everything just yet—but I am the kind of person who likes to live in hope, and who thinks it's easier to deal from a place with a belly full of warmth.*

One night, I'm off the hook. No dinner. We go to a brewery, where we sit along a large bench and eat sliders and fries. Anna has a cider and I have a Kölsch. All the kids are at an age where they can read a menu and stay seated. We play Uno and talk about what is up tomorrow. We've been visiting sites around the park, some of which we find online and some of which we find through various guidebooks and pamphlets left around the cabin. Our daughter is the queen of maps. In a museum, we have to remind her that she is there to look at the art, not the map. But what if the pleasure, for her, is in the map? Or, more precisely, a part of the powerful delight seems to be leading us to where we want to go. The boys are bossy and assertive about the art they want to see. The older one likes things that are flush with color, bright and abstract. The younger likes pottery, furniture, and tapestry. Our daughter leads us through the Philadelphia Museum of Art, through the Minneapolis Institute of Art, pointing her stubby forefinger, its nail painted black, at the color block representing the room we want to find. What would it be like, I wonder, to disrupt her sense of being the youngest, of always having something to prove? I wish I could ask her what she thinks Anna and I should do. Would she be a good older sister? Was I? In the cabins we rent, there are packets of trail maps, and they are the light that draws her, like a moth.

Since the greatest currency in our marriage is solo time, no kids, I offer to take the kids hiking one morning in Shenandoah. Anna is reading an apocalyptic thriller she doesn't want to part with, and besides, she's the first to admit she hates hiking, something she grew up doing with her parents in the mountains of southern Poland. She comes on these trips for the cabin part, not the walking-in-the-woods part. The kids and I arrive at the trail, which has been designated easy by the rating system on the app I use both near home and when we travel, and so we easily make it around the 1.5-mile loop in short order. *Krys*, one of them says, *can we try the medium hike now? That was too short*. My map-loving daughter points in a new direction. Recently I've been thinking that if it works, that if I get pregnant and have another baby, I'll want her to call me Dad. I don't need to stand aside from men anymore. Maybe *Dad* doesn't capture the fullness of me, the totality of my experience and how I live in the world of my family, but so what? It's easy and legible. I don't need to make a statement or to find the perfect, most comfortable thing. I haven't told the kids that I want another baby. Almost no one knows I've been off testosterone for seven months. It is impossible to describe the level of chest-swelling, soaring hope I felt the afternoon I booked a consultation with my fertility doctor. I was working from home, wearing a neat button-down shirt. My computer was arranged to display my bookcase, which I had recently changed so that the books were ordered by spine color. It broke the tension of every work meeting, especially if I joined before the patient and their family but after the school staff was there. *Wow, your books are beautiful*, a teacher or a school nurse would say. Most people at work don't know that I write. I am always walling myself off from other parts of me.

The initial meeting with my doctor was scheduled for my lunch break. It felt so strange, like a bomb dropped in the middle of a boring day. But a good bomb, right? *I am really doing this*, I thought the entire time I spoke with the reproductive endocrinologist who first met me a decade ago, before I had any children. We went over how much sperm we had stored away, and my preference for using few medications and for doing IUI, and we talked about how much time I'd spent on testosterone, and what my periods had been like in the months since I stopped, and what the next few weeks would look like, hopefully some blood work and then right to insemination attempts, if I wanted. We made an appointment for blood work and an exam and I closed my calendar tab and then my computer. On my way to that next step, I placed my hand on the subway window and watched the above and then underground of my city whir by as I entered the next chapter of my life, the last chapter in this saga of family building that had consumed my mid- and late twenties. It was a step forward and a step back. In the appointment that would follow the train ride, the doctor introduced me to my nurse practitioner on our way into the exam room. She said to the nurse practitioner, who would become my tortured patient-portal correspondent over the next few months, *This is Krys. Hopefully you won't be working together long.* The air was light. And then she put the wand into me and found that, subverting all our expectations, I had few follicles growing in either ovary, and maybe the nurse practitioner and I would need to work together quite a bit after all.

The intermediate trail is perhaps intermediate for an adult, or a group of four adults, but it is not intermediate for a man who is a sub-mediocre hiker and his three young children, one of whom is about to start kindergarten, one of whom is about to start second grade, and one of whom is about to start fourth grade. I am carrying a backpack of sunscreen and granola bars and metal water bottles that clink and clank off one another. By the time I realize I have made a mistake bringing them here, the danger is happening now, and my children are precipitously close to the edge of a rock wall that two of them need help traversing. The one son, he keeps getting just far enough ahead to be only within earshot if I'm shouting, and I'm afraid to shout, because I could startle one of the children I'm helping avoid fall off the mountain. But look at them—their movements, their faces—they don't know this is dangerous. In their minds, this is peak Good Dadding, bringing them out here, handing them apples and chocolate before heading up a difficult path.

My children do not know about the anxiety that suffuses most of my days, most of my moments. Although there are times working in the oncology clinic when I've asked myself, Why do something so depressing? Why spend your day emailing back and forth, with increasing fervor and passion, with a school who can't find a bus attendant for a child dying of a brain tumor? Somehow the fact that it isn't the most depressing job I could imagine has helped. To me, working in the pediatric emergency department would be the worst. In the main entrance of the hospital, walking in to get to the clinic, I avert my gaze, looking to the right so I will not see the families waiting, in the ED overflow. *Worse than an adult*

ED? Anna would say. She's haunted by the way she felt, that she absorbed the emergency system's treatment of people, the way the desperately poor and ill were shuffled in and out of waiting rooms and exam rooms and hallways and forced back out the door, into the cold homelessness that awaited them. At least, she surmises, most people in a children's hospital still treat their patients like people.

What I think about are the small-scale accidents, all the catastrophes that could have happened to my children that somehow, miraculously, didn't. The idea that one adult can watch three children who can walk, it's a falsehood. I think about all the times we took them to the lake. The time Anna caught one of them lighting a paper on fire, waving it so close to the curtains. Setting an actual fire, while cooking dinner, tripping halfway into the oven and dropping a mound of corn bread batter directly onto the bottom of the oven. *We're just down the street if you need us*, the firefighter said, looking at the chaos of our family, Anna on the sidewalk half asleep in her pajamas, me corralling three kids on the lawn. A knife on the edge of a counter. Every single time you get in the car with them. You're only dreaming that statistics are on your side. Once, when the boys were babies together, I turned to tie my shoelace before taking them on a walk. They were in the double stroller, and I had forgotten to lock it, and it rolled right into our busy street, coming within inches of being hit by an oncoming car. My distraught face was not enough for the driver. *What is wrong with you?* he kept yelling out the car window. I don't know! What *is* wrong with me? A part of me knew and a part of me didn't, you know? Maybe whatever is wrong with me is the reason we are at this trail's peak and people are looking at me funny. A man approaches. *You came up here all alone, with them?* He looks at my children in their beaten sneakers and baseball caps. I realize that, more than looking at me and the kids, the strangers on the peak were looking behind us, looking for the other adult.

My children sit on a rock and look out. We have made it to a place with an incredible view. All around us trees and cliffs. The kids glisten with summer moisture, tanned by the sun. Anna on the porch with her thriller, waiting for us to come home. Why did I think the way down would be easier? My parents never took me hiking, never took us into nature, not once. Vacation meant a motel pool, a theme park, grandma's house. One time, a resort. I don't know how or why my children and I all make it down the mountain, but we do.

I stink like adrenaline sweat. In the car, they are all *Do you have any snacks left, I need my water bottle, can you turn the music up?* They don't have any access to my interior, and the world, to them, isn't a place you might not be a part of at a moment's notice.

I cook a lot, maybe even more and better than usual, in the months I take the fertility medications to try to make my ovaries cooperate with my desire. It turns out nothing makes me want a baby more than being told I can't have one.

Summer is ending and it's almost fall again. The market near our house is lush with color and fragrance. In addition to my weekly hauls from a big supermarket over the bridge in New Jersey, I find myself at the market touching perfect fruits and vegetables overflowing from wooden crates. It's still the perfect walk from home. I use the last of the summer corn to make huge bowls of corn salad with a dressing made of mayonnaise and sour cream and loads of lime juice, crumbled cotija cheese, chili powder, and pickled onions. It's even better for leftovers, which Anna and I split and take in pint containers to our jobs. It's a *Smitten Kitchen* recipe, and I serve it strewn across a platter like Perelman does. I eat the end-of-summer tomatoes in slices, salted, standing over the sink, my legs spread out so no juices hit my pants. I make a lime-and-jalapeño slaw out of a brilliant-purple cabbage, colors I can't believe exist in this dark haze. I make soup: squash and tomato and chicken and carrot. I make Perelman's pumpkin bread and pumpkin bread again and butterscotch pudding popsicles and butterscotch pudding popsicles again. At the end of my workdays, my hands are shaking from attending to a computer screen and writing the words *wheelchair lift*, *cancer predisposition syndrome*, *craniotomy*, *optic pathway glioma*. In the pictures I take, my food looks beautiful and perfect, but I am broken.

The cooking is happening for the same reasons as before—I have three children and they are hungry, I have a wife who is hungry, I know how to do it, I need to do it—but also for new, different reasons. I am cooking to save my life, it seems. The edges of things feel softened, like I am not a part of the same sharp reality anymore. I only feel myself when I am here, frosting a cake, cutting an onion into a steady, even dice. The service looks like it is for someone else, but above all, it is about me.

Nearly a decade ago, I said I would never carry another baby. Making the first one pushed me to the edge of myself, and when I came back, I was ready for a new life. A man's life. The baby I made got older and older, and eventually we hardly ever talked about the fact that he was mine and not Anna's. There were days, weeks even, when I didn't think of it once. Sometimes there were the jokes. *Why are you so ugly?* I'd ask him, looking right into his beautiful blue eyes. *My genetics*, he'd say automatically. I assumed his friends, his coaches, his teachers, didn't know, and if they did, they wouldn't care. There isn't a way to talk about it that isn't complicated, and who wants to complicate life?

I always tell friends who are expecting a baby how, once your kid is older, no one cares where or how you gave birth or what you fed your infant. You are the only one left with the memory of giving birth. You remember the little bits of blood and vernix that cling to your newborn's head, you remember your head between your legs after someone helps you to the bathroom for the first time after you've gotten the baby out, when you sit on the toilet feeling like you've had all the life sucked out of your body, so much that it's effortful to pee. You are the only one who remembers opening a can of formula in the middle of a long night, who knows whether your baby took their first bite of solid food with relish or pushed it right back out with their little, unpracticed tongue. Your baby doesn't remember any of this. And no one else cared the way you did.

My son turned five, six, seven, eight, nine. We talked about how he liked many of the foods I liked, how he liked food the way his brother and sister didn't. We talked about his face, which is my sister's face, and his hair, which is my hair. There was this tension I felt about it, about being a man who had carried a baby, about doing it before transition, when no one, not even me, fully understood what it was that I had done. Was waiting to transition until after this big event cowardly? It was the great drama of my life. I didn't move on from him for many years, and so I didn't pine for babies, especially not for making another of my own. Until I did. This desire is one of the things about being a person I find hardest to explain, my willingness to throw away the stability of my life to chase it. I wanted it the way people want to climb big mountains or swim around continents, I wanted to have a bodily experience that would help me feel truly alive, truly real. Why did I need to have a baby to feel like a real person, a real man? I was someone who had taken one of the essential facts of my life, that I was born a girl, and bent reality to my will. I wanted to do it again, but the universe was saying, resoundingly, no.

Maybe I never wanted a stable life and now I am stuck in a family and there's only so much I can do to shake myself awake. Maybe my will is only so strong and it has bent over the years to the knowledge that Anna wants one more child. Maybe it's all those things. But to get there, I have to bend myself to the will of fertility doctors and I have to spend time and money on something that may not work out. I am chasing after something I know from experience can and will hurt me, and I am doing it with all my might.

One night, I don't make the kids dinner, I grab them big greasy pizza slices from around the corner and, later, after they have gone to bed, I make me and Anna giant steak salads, an embarrassment of fat and abundance and color in big bowls that we eat in front of the television late at night. Arugula, blue cheese, rib eye, hunks of pepper and cucumber. And we go to bed full of meat and greens and the bread I served on the side, but I am still hungry: the sex we have in the months as I work to accept it's over for me, that it won't work, that I had a baby at twenty-six and then became infertile in a way medications won't help, it's so good and so frequent. Night after night, Anna tops me, something that has happened only infrequently in the past. I am on my back, I am on my knees, all these new ways to be in the body I thought I knew better than I did. And it makes sense—I have given my body completely to my doctor and nurse practitioner, I will sign any consent form and come to any visit and do anything they tell me, I want people to tell me what to do to fix me, and giving of myself completely in bed feels natural in this time of self-obliteration.

Everyone gets to the point where they start to phone in their own life, and this is mine: Perelman's 2018 recipe for quick pasta and chickpeas only uses something fresh if you count garlic as a fresh ingredient. She calls for fresh rosemary, but who can be bothered, I just use the sandpapery flecks in a little plastic tube. It is filling and takes twenty minutes to make. When I am scrubbing the pot and, then, washing my tired hands, the scent of garlic and rosemary remains. It's a reminder to me that I am still in the world I was in before, when I decided to try. After a short list of ingredients, which I quickly memorize, the recipe is just 176 words. Which is good, because, as I'm sure my children can tell, young as they are, I don't have the patience to listen to much more than that.

In *In Vitro: On Longing and Transformation*, Isabel Zapata writes about sitting in the fertility clinic waiting room, longing to ask the other women how they ended up there, but feeling like she can't. IVF is something that few people talk about.

Zapata focuses on the otherworldliness of the technological landscape in her clinic, writing about *colossal leaps forward in the controversial territories of embryo vitrification, endometrial scratching, gestational surrogacy, male pregnancy, and predetermining the sex of the fetus.* I observe these things, too, but it is the mundanity of the clinic's details: the dingy hallway leading to its elevator, the way everyone who gets on with me early in the morning presses the same button for the eleventh floor, the procession of men who step off the elevator with women, only to turn toward the sperm collection room.

Zapata writes, *The clinic exists out of time.* In needing to go to the clinic, I find a whole new set of hours before I go to work, before my children are even awake. In the beginning, I don't know whether to tell them where I am going, because I ultimately don't know what will happen, and they are only children. I schedule my blood draws for 7 a.m. I don't talk to, don't look at anyone as I walk through Kensington in the early hours. I wear one of the good masks because I could get pregnant this month or the next or the next. Her body is already worth more than mine. It's hot and only a little bit dark and I stand alone on the subway platform in my khakis and my T-shirt with my big checkered backpack. I have a work shirt folded neatly inside, pressed against my laptop. I wear sneakers every day. I could be going anywhere on the train.

I get off at Eleventh Street. Floods of nurses in bright-blue scrubs head toward the hospital in anticipation of change of shift. At the fertility clinic check-in counter, the receptionists always look happy to see me. They don't have to look at what I'm writing on the sign-in sheet to know my name because I am here every day in a sea of women. I always bring a book in case I need to wait. The phlebotomists like my tattoos and tell me about the books they are reading. I am an easy patient. I don't have questions. I have good veins. Blood runs out of me. When I lie back in the exam room, my stomach lurches every time.

Sometimes my knees and thighs shake involuntarily the moment before my doctor sticks the ultrasound wand inside me. She is a blunt woman, but there is nothing blunt about her expression. I can tell by the way she looks in my eyes that she feels for me as she does this to me again and again, multiple times a week for months on end. When the parade of students always following her look at me, they look afraid to mess something up, even though they're not expected to do anything, even to speak. They are only there to watch me.

I want to remember what the screen looked like when she did this before and my ovaries were full, full of follicles, young and healthy and ready to make a baby for the first time, but I don't. How was I supposed to know to hold on?

When she took care of me back then, I was focused on other things. They seemed so important. I wanted to be different. I wanted to be a man. I wanted a beard and bigger shoulders. I wanted a man's voice. I never wanted to be called a dyke again. I wanted the words: *son*, *brother*. I wanted to grow up. I wanted to look serious in sweaters. I wanted to splurge on better glasses. I wanted a couch that wasn't from IKEA. I know I'm infertile, and I don't remember what I felt like before I knew because I didn't know to appreciate the way I was before. The doctor met me before Anna and I had any children at all. How does she go on like this, year after year, replicating this same compassion? She has had the same job for decades and I am reaching the end of my compassion after only a year at mine. I have become, in just a few short months, someone narrowly focused on my infertility. Instead of asking how I am doing, the doctor comments on my sneakers, which are off my feet and placed beneath the chair that holds my folded clothes. *Which ones did you wear today?* She likes the bolder ones. The hot-pink Vans. The Vans with the flowers. She says she does not know anyone who owns more pairs of Vans than I do. She says her feet are too old for Vans. She is calling me young. She asks what I am reading and I say the name of a memoir. I don't know if she knows I am a writer. I tend to hope no one does. She knows I work at a desk in an oncology clinic and that the children's hospital insurance is paying my exorbitant, disgustingly selfish medical bills. *I don't much like memoir*, she says. *Have you read any good novels lately?*

I am to take one pill per day for five days to try to convince my ovaries to work. On the morning I take the first one, I make the kids hot breakfast, chocolate chip muffins and scrambled eggs, and Anna drives them to my parents' for a few days so that she and I can spend some time together. I put the extra muffins in a sack on the passenger seat for my mother.

I don't make dinner these few days. We go out to a nice restaurant, then a dive bar. I drink too much. A sazerac and IPA in a can. I want to think about anything except the medicine. There aren't any dishes in the sink at home because we get our coffees out and eat lunches at work. With no kids around, we don't have to run the washer and the dryer every damn minute we're at home. We text all day about seeing each other after work, and we only call my mother and our children once a day. I take a day off. I pick her up from work. I think I'm gonna be so suave and romantic showing up at the birth center unannounced, but there's a train delay so long that I feel intensely bonded to the other forty or so people on the platform by the time we finally board. I text Anna to let her know please not to leave work on time because I was going to surprise her but then there was this delay. *Wait for me, I'm almost at the stop. Surprise!* God, I am such a silly little man. Nothing I do works out the way I planned it. We split a barbecue pizza in the park. We go to one bar and another. The hot flashes from the fertility medication begin low in my torso and rise up through my chest, into my neck, all around my head. I can feel my ears heat up. When I take this medication and the next one, too, I am aflame the whole time and for weeks after.

The medicines don't work. The emails from the clinic come like clockwork in the middle of my workdays. The nurse practitioner is sorry and she's sorry and she's sorry again.

And then, a wave of static. I lose days and weeks in real time and in memory. But I know there's never a day I don't get out of bed, never a day I can't make dinner. Obligation animates me, but my efforts go into doing the basics. I fold the kids' socks and fold their underwear and make toast with butter and cinnamon sugar and pesto mozzarella sandwiches with the crusts cut off. Again and again, I remember opening the first packet of fertility pills, convinced they ruined me for good. That sound of foil and plastic ripping, a swig of water to wash it down. I remember only one day clearly:

I am walking from the subway to work and it hits me. I'm in danger. Around me, hundreds of cars driving like crazy headed into the children's hospital and the adult hospitals and all the outpatient clinics that make up this corner of town. So many sick. Every lane of every road is always packed with patients and families and doctors headed in and out of garages and valet lots. Every single person I see has a hospital badge. All around, horns beeping. An ambulance blaring, then another. I am not safe. I am not pregnant and I won't be because my body doesn't work. I'm not myself anymore. I waited too long to decide what I wanted. I can't collect any thoughts except wanting to lie in the road. The feeling slams me like never before. I don't want to see if I'll still feel this way tomorrow. My body is hot again, even my fingertips, even my feet. I see myself from above standing in the crosswalk a second too long trying to decide what to do. A hospital security guard is waving his arms wildly to help direct traffic. The women going into the hospital where I work wear gray scrubs, and the ones going into the adult hospital wear navy blue. Waves of workers. They are reconstructing the adult emergency room and there are cones and cranes all over the place. I consider going to the ER instead of to my office, but then what? Every ER in the city is slammed. There is a pandemic. I'll be there all day and all night and Anna will have to call out of work and call someone else in. How to even explain what is wrong with me? I never think about how people love me and want me to live. I don't think about how insane it is, to want to bring someone else into the world I feel I have to leave right now, today, before I am supposed to be at my desk in the oncology clinic at 8:30 sharp. I only think that the fridge is nearly empty and who will make dinner if I'm not at home?

After that day, it's on to IVF, on to Anna's eggs. It is through Zoom that my fertility doctor looks at me with naked compassion and tells me that I don't have to keep trying. *You have the best egg donor there is sitting right next to you*, she says, with a faint, sympathetic smile.

It is time to reset my dream of domestic bliss. Anna is nearly forty and I have the health insurance now and there's no time to think through all the ways I will feel. I want to carry a baby so badly, and Anna doesn't, doesn't want to take time off work, doesn't want to be the one the baby cries out for in the night. On one of our walks, she regards me frankly: *It's sort of a shit-or-get-off-the-pot moment*, she says. *Are we going to have a baby or not?*

In the introduction to her third cookbook, *Smitten Kitchen Keepers*, Perelman writes, *I don't mean to be melodramatic, but I think this is the book I was always meant to write. Given that it's my third cookbook, this is a bit awkward. It would be like declaring a new child the one you got right, while your first two glare at you from across the room.*

She does not have a third child, but this still tickles me. It would be silly not to see a new child as the possibility of revision. Will I be able to, after all this, tune in for the experience?

In the photograph from Christmas Eve, my three children have their arms around one another in front of my blue dutch oven and a board covered in cheese, crackers, and fruit. Inside the pot, Short Rib Onion Soup from *Smitten Kitchen*. My children all need haircuts, and they look very happy. They're all wearing red. The caption: *very thankful today for these goofy kids, all their help in the kitchen today, and the wonderful meal we were able to share this evening*. Then, a Christmas tree emoji. Christmas Day, Anna will begin injecting thousands of dollars of hormones into her stomach fat to stimulate hyper-ovulation in the hopes of creating another baby. But I don't tell people that. I only send a link to the recipe, texting with a friend who sees my post about whether the soup was worth the effort. I don't know anyone who cooks who doesn't cook Perelman's recipes. I egg my friend on. Make the soup! All those hours and steps: browning the short ribs, caramelizing the onions, making the croutons-and-gruyère lid. What I didn't say, but maybe should have, is yes, anything is worth the effort if you have the disaster of your life to avoid.

The Short Rib Onion Soup recipe, which Perelman calls *peak December cozy luxury*, calls for three pounds of short ribs and three pounds of onions. In a time when recipe blogs have become clogged with advertisements and descriptions filled with search-engine-friendly key words but entirely lacking character, she can really, really write. In a way, her nearly two decades of blogging and her cookbooks combine into an extended, enrapturing, memoir of dailiness and devotion to making dinner. There's something maddening about the political idea that we should want to have a beer with our politicians, but that metric to me feels entirely appropriate for a food blogger. I think that if we were neighbors, Perelman and I might get along over backyard beers. Over the years, she has responded to many of the comments on her blog, answering questions, commenting on tips, even just joking around. In her introduction to Short Rib Onion Soup, which went live just a few days before I made it, she relays a story about going to a friend's house briefly and being met with the presence of a big pot of chicken chili. *Despite not planning to stay,* she writes, *we inhaled a bowl in her yard before heading back out again and I have not stopped thinking about it since, hospitality on a you-never-know level.* Something in me shifted, reading this. Was there a world in which I could entertain again, invite someone over for anything other than holding a hot cup of tea or a beer in my backyard? It was a moment of clarity because, for once, I was thinking about something other than the baby I was failing to have.

In Poland, Anna says, Christmas Eve was the real celebration—the family dinner, the waiting for Santa. I've never met anyone from her extended family, only her parents and her one surviving brother. Her life there was spent mostly in an apartment complex, traveling to its outskirts for school, and to the mountains in the south on occasional summer trips. In my family, Christmas Day was the main affair, and my mother cooked basically a replica of Thanksgiving dinner for the family. The focus was on the presents, mountains of gifts under the tree and under relatives' arms as they came to visit. A holiday of things rather than food.

Now, we sigh small, secret relief breaths when Anna's holiday schedule comes out and she's working the night before or the night of, and we have to tell my family we're going to opt out. These are the things warring inside me, the want to be the type of person connected to people outside my immediate family, and the dread I feel having to leave my house. I like to read the women who cook to entertain because there's an aspirational note to it, something I could be, if the world and my anxiety would quiet down and cooperate.

Kristen Radtke writes, *I fear that through the act of posting about my own life, I'm also fooling myself into believing it reflects what it's like to lie inside it—just as I've sometimes told the same story so many times that the telling overtakes my memory itself.*

We sit around the table spreading cheese on crackers and eating bowls of this impossibly fussy and rich soup. Before we take a bite, we sprinkle perfectly minced chives on top. And I click *post* so the world can see this gorgeous meal, my gorgeous children.

I need to find a way to come back to things that are tangible, because, if I have the baby, I'll have to integrate that fact into my life, I'll have to go on living and doing.

Perelman writes, of a simple chocolate cake I have since made a dozen times, a chocolate cake I love,

> *I wanted a slice of chocolate cake with swirls of chocolate frosting and probably some sprinkles and the sprinkles, so help them, better be rainbow. Except the word "wanted" doesn't accurately describe the craving; it was suddenly everything.*

The night 2021 goes away, I make dinner. And I make chocolate cake. In a video, my son stands next to me as I pour the hot frosting, exhaling breathily, in plain awe, as it hits the warm cake. I can do that. The candles say 2-0-2-2. Held breath, a wish.

In her recipe for perfect lasagna, Deb Perelman uses Anne Burrell's recipe for bolognese. It's one of those things she gravitates toward, more a method than a recipe. She is not Martha or Ina not only because of the aforementioned lack of neat, domestic perfection, but also because she loves to share things like this sauce, which is a vibe and an experience more than a precise formula. It takes hours and hours, and the sauce is dark and wine rich, gut busting in the best way. This is my go-to.

But on the first day of January, I want to try something new, so I make Marcella Hazan's bolognese. Like my standard, this is a recipe where you do stuff for a while, a moderate while, and then you walk away and let it cook for many hours. Bolognese is one of the few things I find consistently strong enough to drown out the smell my house—of dog, of too-old laundry sitting forgotten in the washer again, of endless rounds of cinnamon toast I make for the kids each morning. Bolognese makes me want to step outside my house just to step back inside and smell it again. This recipe feels fresher, the vegetables chopped instead of annihilated in the food processor, the wine white instead of red. Milk stirred in early, then bubbled away. What does it even mean anymore to want something from a year? This recipe has no garlic, which I find quietly appalling, but I follow it exactly, promised by the internet that in five hours, give or take, an incident of pure magic will occur in my kitchen. I watch videos of multiple people making the recipe, wondering if I, too, should make fresh pappardelle. My children are in the living room lounging and their mother is asleep upstairs. I have promised my children that when the sauce is finally bubbling—*at the laziest of simmers, with just an intermittent bubble breaking through to the surface*—I will go running and they can watch a movie, so of course I cannot, should not, make fresh pasta. I stir in the wine, then, when that is gone, the chopped tomatoes. My sister is coming for dinner, for the bolognese, and is staying overnight because in the morning Anna will have her eggs retrieved. Telling my sister made it real, that this is something we want, that it is what we have chosen to do because I am not fertile. That is how I say it to her: *I am not fertile*. It has been all those years since we had the other kids and yet we still want. The hunger is still in us. I remember the shock of opening the dutch oven that Christmas morning—it was a gift from my mother—and balking at the thought that these were the kinds of things that lasted forever. What was my forever?

When I buy myself kitchen supplies, I never buy things that last. In Target, I stood before the nonstick pan sets and I thought, These will last but not too long, and put the set into my cart. As the Teflon flakes, I think about how I have outlived another thing. The cheap pans are all dinged up, need to be replaced. But my family wants me to persist. There was the dutch oven, and then, a year or two later, a matching cast-iron enamel baking dish. Two all-clad pans from my godmother came after that. What do they know that I don't? My mother bought me other kitchen luxuries—my stand mixer, my food processor—but those lasted many years and then died, or broke. The pot is different. It was never going to break unless I broke it.

The next day, I make chicken soup. I think about how Perelman says chicken soup can't solve everything, but I know Anna thinks it can do what medicine cannot. The Chicken Soup Clinic, she jokes, is the business we will open together. We will operate on the edge of a college campus. Our patients will be lonely college students away from home for their first illness. She will hand out Motrin and blankets and I will ladle chicken soup into paper cups.

I am not allowed into the surgical center where the procedure will happen. I am to remain in the parking lot—*on the premises*, the nurse told Anna on the phone—the entire time. This is the protocol with sickness still everywhere.

When discussing this procedure with Anna, I cannot help but center myself. I can barely stand the thought of continuing to live *with* her, so what would I do if she died, and what if she died trying to give me eggs for this stupid, selfish enterprise of creating a fourth baby? She laughs. *It's only conscious sedation*, she says. *Want to hear about it?* We are in our bed, on our sides, and it has been a week of trying to avoid putting my hands anywhere where the fresh swelling is happening, still happening, and now in its most intense phase. Her ovaries are being forced into creating so much of what I lack. Each morning, Anna goes to the clinic's office and is shown pictures of the growing. Lying in bed, she tells me about sedating people in the ED. Exactly how the drugs are given. Unlike me, Anna looks middle aged, with her graying hair, hands thin and tough from endless washing and sanitizing in the emergency department and at the birth center where she works. It has taken me many years to understand that at her jobs, she spends time in ways I can never really understand.

She is wearing scrubs. She is in a hallway. She is in a room. There is a place called the nurses' station. There are machines, tubes. My mind fills in the gaps between her stories, but somewhere in me I know that none of it is correct. Since Anna became a nurse, the words she says about the work she does could mean nearly anything. So she explains the egg retrieval as patiently as she can. She wants me to know because it's important, because I'm afraid. She explains to me the difference between conscious sedation and general anesthesia. *I am always surprised by how much propofol some of these old ladies in the ER need*, she says. She laughs. She looks light, happy. She adjusts, grimacing at the weight of everything inside her. Even in this state, she is trying to solve my insomnia. She is trying to solve the fact that I cannot have another baby. Everything to Anna is either a joke or a problem to solve, or both. After a while of silence, I ask her what she's feeling and she says she is feeling nothing, but it seems like it's nothing in a good way. What is that like? There are moments, when I am in the kitchen, when I am making dinner, when I come close. If I am on my feet, if I am hearing food sizzling while stirring a sauce, if I am laying out all the ingredients I will need for the next phase of the meal, it grows quiet, but never completely quiet. Anna hesitates, then asks what about me, what am I feeling, and I say, *I feel everything*.

I am sitting in the parking lot of a surgical center of a day both doomed and special. There is usually nothing special about the second day of the year. Nothing fresh at all. Listen, that pasta yesterday was good. We all ate it, with heavily buttered baguette, with brussels sprouts salted and roasted deeply and tossed with a bit of balsamic vinegar. The sauce was meaty and rich and yet I like my old recipe better. Sitting in the parking lot, facing days of bolognese leftovers, I wonder about the fortune of this year. In the parking lot, I want to watch the sun come up, but the day grinds in hard and grim, muted gray imperceptibly replacing the black in a creeping, undramatic way. No color I can see. And suddenly it is no longer early morning, it is the full-blown day when the eggs will be removed, the embryos will be made, the thing that will become my child may happen. Anna is inside the surgical center and I am scared. I know it's a low-risk procedure, I know all that. I know how unlikely she is to meet harm, how unlikely I am to meet harm, how likely it is the world will keep spinning with us on it. We are likely to grow old, as likely as anyone. But what if I do this thing, step up to the edge of the diving board, and then am told I'm not able to jump in? If all works out, I will have a frozen embryo implanted in me in a month. For the first time since I decided to have the baby, I feel she might really happen. Is this worse in the car or would it have been worse if we were doing this in a time when I could sit in the waiting room? I am in the driver's seat reading a romance novel, but when I cannot concentrate on that, I close my eyes and picture the soup I promised I would make tonight. From the bolognese I have carrots and celery and onions in the house, and I bought chicken on the bone. There are four parmesan rinds in a baggie in the freezer. A bunch of dill, a box of pasta. I washed out my dutch oven to use it again. All in my house agree: chicken soup ought to be very brothy. The kids know where we are, they know why their aunt is there, but they do not know anything about how I am feeling. Her solution is to give me her eggs, and my solution is soup. You get near the pot, you open it up, and it takes you over.

Alison

In the photo, the baby rests with her eyes open, looking in the direction of the phone taking the picture, but in the unfocused way they have in the first few weeks, the exertion of looking intently at something, even something close, even their parent, too much for their developing retinas. She is two weeks old. She is wearing a onesie with Eric Carle–style food items, the one from that indulgent page of *The Very Hungry Caterpillar*, one sausage, one piece of cherry pie, one lollipop, on and on. She doesn't look like me, of course, and she also doesn't look like her mother, not yet. She looks like something that's just emerged from underwater, though it's been some time now. Her eyes are wrinkled and her head looks heavy, weighted into my bed. Behind her, a crib, one of its slatted sides removed, is bungee corded to the side of the bed, creating a sort of mega bed. This isn't safe sleep, but it's what works. At night, I pull the baby close to me, our sides touching, her lying on her back, my arm wrapped around the top of her head. It's clear nobody's been sleeping in the crib, which, in this captured moment, contains a large novel, a case of diaper wipes, a changing pad, cloth diapers, a remote for a standing fan, a crumpled baby onesie, and, most importantly, a laptop open to a cooking video. In the video, Alison Roman wears a tight olive T-shirt, gold hoop earrings, and a folded blue apron tied at the waist. She is holding a packet of yeast. The text, partially obscured by a baby's head, says something about bubbly, something about activated. This is obviously her kitchen, more cluttered than the typical content creator's kitchen but less cluttered than Claire Saffitz's. The last few weeks have changed me, and instead of being charmed by Roman's space, I question why she didn't bother to clean. Why couldn't I bother to clear off this bed before photographing my daughter?

Of all the food celebrities who have gotten me through this time of global upheaval, of upheaval of my family and my gender and my life, Roman is the only one about whom there's any major controversy. The recipe that hooked me was the cauliflower pasta, resplendent with cream and pecorino cheese, topped with breadcrumbs. My office mate from the clinic clued me in to it, to Roman as an entity, setting me down a path of bucatini with anchovies, bean stews, viral recipes that made me feel a part of something. Ultimately, I settled on one recipe as my make-again-and-again: the brown butter buttermilk cake from her 2017 cookbook *Dining In*, which I received for Christmas. The simple cake, made in a single nine-inch cake pan, is tart and soft and buttery, glazed lightly with buttermilk and brown butter and powdered sugar. Roman instructs you to line the pan with parchment, and does it in a messy way that creates beautiful divots where the parchment cuts into the expanding cake. When I made it again and again, in the year we were stuck at home, we would each eat a slice after dinner and a slice with breakfast the next day, with a pile of scrambled eggs, giving in to the need we had for daily indulgence.

When Roman blasted Marie Kondo and Chrissy Teigen for selling branded products, an outburst many considered racist, it didn't feel like giving up anything to stop paying attention to her, to stop bookmarking the videos. I had, after all, acquired the cookbook, so I could make the cake, which I was close to memorizing anyway, and anything else in the spare and beautiful cookbook, whenever I wanted, without giving Roman more of my money or giving her my attention after she had fucked up and refused, to my mind and many others', to apologize sufficiently. When I make the cauliflower pasta now, from memory, I know the alterations that work for me, upping the pasta from twelve to sixteen ounces, roasting the cauliflower on a sheet pan at a high heat, then mixing it with the shallots and cream, instead of sautéing the cauliflower in the same pan as the alliums. At some point, I sent Anna an email with directions to make the pasta, which I wrote without looking at the original. There's a degree to which, once you alter something enough, you begin to forget where it came from in the first place.

In These Trying Times, we reach for the things that get us through our monotonous days. Zoom calls with family. A perfectly risen sourdough loaf. And of course, Twitter gossip about popular-but-niche food personalities, Jaya Saxena wrote for *Eater* soon after it happened. Roman isn't the only thing my coworker and I discuss. Between meetings, we chat Sohla El-Waylly, Samin Nosrat, Carla Lalli Music, we discuss cookie recipes and whether Coke is better from a fountain or a bottle, I pine after the tehina milkshakes you can get a few blocks away from the office, we discuss our neighborhoods and our kids and our dogs, we discuss school board policy and upcoming elections. We have other things to worry about.

And yet Roman remains, even after I leave the hospital. When I make a Roman recipe, I text my coworker: *Making Alison Roman's baked ziti for dinner*. It isn't the exact recipe that sticks with me, so at some point, it may not have even been fair to say it's her recipe I am making, but the technique of stirring a big glug of cream into the ricotta, which smooths it out, makes it break less while cooking. Texting my office mate, more a reach-out than a confession, became a way to feel like I was still the me who had walked into that gleaming hospital entryway, who had sat in the main lobby waiting for someone from my department to greet me at the door, in my new badge, with my name and the word *ONCOLOGY* written beneath it. I was the me who had sat at a desk before there was a pandemic and considered a life in which I stopped making changes, stopped moving from place to place and from job to job, really sat and focused on something other than learning to cook new recipes. I've had four children and there is always a dawning realization that you can never go back to who you were, and maybe a wobbly moment when you feel you have made a mistake, but never before have I felt so untethered from the people around me, and if Roman helps me stay grounded, I have to accept that.

My office mates were some of the only people who knew I was trying to have another baby. I'm not saying they were perfect, or close, but the drama of my everyday life was so small, so low stakes, compared to the drama playing out in every patient's life, and so I thought they would respond how they did: neutrally, supportively, steadily. I didn't ask for anything, but being able to talk about it was enough.

Congrats on fulfilling your dream of not working here anymore, said the card one of them gave me on the last day in my office.

The truth is that I circle back around to Roman because once I have the baby, I'm angry and I'm upset and I need a comeback. And I want to see if Roman is making hers. There's something, too, about the spitefulness I know in my bones she may exhibit once I press *play*. In my daily life, I'm everything Roman isn't: reserved, conciliatory, relentlessly positive with everyone but my closest friends. But I can't martial any of those sentiments now. Lying in my bed with the baby, I watch Alison Roman again. And she doesn't disappoint. She starts her video "The Best Meatball Recipe" with a brief prelude, an aside to the staff with her in her kitchen: *Should we predict all the complaints? Because I can tell you what they're going to be: She's cooking with her ring! Why is she cooking with that shirt? Her pants are weird! I hate her voice!*

She begins discussing the recipe at hand. *I don't always start from being inspired by something great. I am often inspired by something bad. Such is the case with these meatballs.*

It's not till nearly minute eight of the video when she tells viewers the meatballs' story. She and a guy she was dating went to their friends' apartment. The friends served Roman and her boyfriend terrible meatballs. The next day, he abruptly broke up with her, and her friends joke that it had to be the meatballs. *This is essentially therapy*, Roman says. Then, quieter: *I did skip last week.*

The cameraman asks if the breakup was really out of nowhere. Roman admits a breakup is never really out of nowhere. *I was ignoring the signs*, she says. *He shall remain nameless*, Roman adds a few moments later. *He's honestly not even important enough, uh, for me to mention ever again.* I wish I could speak so dismissively of the things that are hurting me, but I can't. In the weeks after my daughter's birth, I can barely say the words out loud. So I watch Roman: brothy beans, potato leek soup. I stay in bed beyond when it hurts to get out of bed and go downstairs, because though I can't stand the staleness of my room, I can't stand the hustle and bustle of the rest of the house to an even greater extent. *Move over, I love her*, Anna says as she scoots into bed with me and the baby to watch Roman make slow-roasted salmon. Anna doesn't mean she likes to cook Roman's recipes. She means she likes to watch.

For eighteen days after I give birth, I do not make dinner. The best meal I eat, I eat again and again: simple chicken soup a friend brings over in purple quart-size jars. She tells me that her husband's feedback is that this soup has too many potatoes, but I could not disagree more. They are perfectly cooked and the broth is mild, not too salty, and rich with chicken flavor.

"I Love Boiled Potatoes," a subheading in Roman's *Dining In* reads. *One of the strangest and most useful things I keep on hand in the refrigerator*, Roman writes, *is a bowl of small, waxy boiled potatoes. In the fridge, they quietly await their destiny*: Smashed potatoes? Hashes? Potato salad? I already miss the usefulness of small things like this, of having something on hand to whip up. I am reliant on Anna for everything, and for others who send and bring over food. Anna heats up the soup and puts fresh pasta into it each time she serves me some, and she toasts me hoagie rolls out of a plastic bag and slathers them with butter. I wolf down every meal she brings to me in bed—potatoes and carrots, hunks and shreds of chicken breast burning my throat. I can't slow down enough not to get burned. I have never been so hungry. Grease coats my mouth, and breadcrumbs flake into my baby's hair.

The friend makes the soup a second time and brings me more. She comes over with a bag of my favorite bagels and coffee, and Anna calls me down to sit with her. I descend the steps gingerly, holding the baby and holding my insides together. I have barely left my bedroom, barely left my bed. I've been spending time with the kids by watching movies we've seen before, and yet I still can't follow what is happening. *Richie*

Rich might as well be a physics lecture. I did not know the friend was coming. And that is when I know that Anna really is worried about me, that she does not think I'm getting any better. She guessed, correctly, that I would say I wasn't up for seeing anyone, not even this woman I have texted with every day for a decade. My body is healing, slowly but surely, but I'm sinking deeper into something dark. And now Anna has called in a witness. There's the baby blues and then there's whatever this is. I nurse the baby and I hope the friend will not ask to hold her and she doesn't, but eventually I pass her across the coffee table so I can prepare my bagel with two hands. Once she is out of my hands, I feel intense freedom. I make Anna's bagel too. This extends my minutes alone. These free hands. And I remember back when I prepared a bagel for Anna after she had our first baby, I am right in that moment ten years ago and we are at a coffee shop near our old apartment and Anna is also not okay. She cries when the baby cries, which is a lot. Sleep when the baby sleeps, cry when the baby cries. She was skeptical that coming to the coffee shop was a good idea, because what if the baby gets upset? *So what if he does?* I ask her. I am not postpartum. I'm just a guy with a baby he wanted. I confidently clothe the baby in outside clothes and hand the baby carrier out with a question on my face: *You or me?* She wants as little to do with the baby as possible, while I cradle him whenever I can, all day and night, his fluffy black hair and fresh smell, like he lived inside of somebody really just a few days ago. *Why does he cry so much?* she asks again and again. *He's a baby*, I say. My son. I take a picture of Anna holding the baby across the coffee shop table because this is my dream, me and her and a baby, at the same coffee shop I came to just a few weeks before, during her early labor, by myself, leaving her at home moaning on the couch, old episodes of *ER* playing in the background, an unsuccessful distraction. We never say the words *postpartum depression* and we won't say them for years. We say *tired*, we say *it's hard to cope*.

My friend holds my new baby, my so-many-years-later fourth baby, and I split my bagel with shaking, hungry hands and I put cream cheese on both halves and I eat it, slowly, watching my friend watch me. When this friend had her first child, we barely knew each other. She was someone I said hello to at the gym where we both worked out. When I was very pregnant with my first, and she was newly pregnant with hers, she stood over me as I lay on the floor in a pool of my own sweat and talked to me about working out while pregnant. I don't know why—I don't tend to put myself out there—but when she had her baby, I texted her to hang out. She kept deferring and deferring until the cold, rainy day in January when I told her firmly I would meet her at a coffee shop a block from her house. I showed up with my two baby boys, one in a stroller, one in a wrap, my umbrella being whipped every which way by the wind, and I watched her cross the street with her baby pressed against her under her husband's enormous coat as rain pounded them both. In the shop, my children did not act their best. My first, who was a toddler, walked around on the rain-slick wooden floor, tripping over his own feet. My second, an infant just a few months older than the new baby across the table, cried for my breast milk, and so I nursed as stealthily as I could in this coffee shop across from this near stranger. My friend sat wide-eyed with her six-week-old baby and said it would never be easy for her like it was for me.

Years later on my couch, I take my baby back from her after my bagel is gone and breastfeed again. Anna puts the soup in the refrigerator and sees my friend out the door and I am alone again.

In 2013, when I first gave birth, I completed the scale in my son's pediatrician's office. I remember juggling the baby, who needed feeding and changing and soothing, and a clipboard with a piece of paper I was to fill out. Was I a little more emotionally wobbly than usual? Sure. But I was able to laugh and see the funny side of things, I looked forward to things with enjoyment, and I was never so unhappy that I had difficulty sleeping. The pediatrician came into the office, glanced at the sheet that I handed her without a hint of worry or shame, and smiled widely at me.

Nearly ten years later, I am in the bed where I had my daughter, trying not to sprinkle everything-bagel dust all over her head while Anna reads the scale to me off her phone. The pediatrician office's remote portal, a new invention in the years between my two births, now contains, as part of its pre-check-in steps, the Edinburgh Postnatal Depression Scale, which has been used increasingly by primary care practitioners around the world since its development the year I was born.

The scale doesn't diagnose anything, just identifies whether depressive symptoms are present in the ~~mother~~ person completing the scale.

10. *The thought of harming myself has occurred to me:*
Yes, quite often
Sometimes
Hardly ever
Never

I would say, and then a pause. I consider. *Sometimes.*

Okay, Anna says. *I'm going to mark* never.

Because, she says, and then she takes her own pause. *Because that's the right answer.*

Psychologist John Cox, who studied the scale's use across multiple populations, wrote that *the sensitivity of item 10 ("the thought of harming myself has occurred to me") was not separately established, but any mother scoring above zero on this item should be carefully assessed.*

Other than this time, when she is reading robotically off a small screen, Anna doesn't ask how I'm coping. What would be the point? It's our fourth round doing all this; she, too, had one baby who made her happy and one who made her depressed. My new daughter has full, pink cheeks and blue eyes, and she's losing what little hair she had on the night she was born, just ten minutes before my forty-first week of pregnancy would have begun. I like the way my daughter's squidgy, wrinkly arms feel against me when we nurse skin to skin under a blanket, and at night I sleep with her flat on her back next to me, my arm reaching around her protectively in an upside-down U. Sometimes when she is sleeping and I am awake I touch her lips with the rough edges of my fingers, shocked that a part of a living thing can be so soft that it's almost impossible for my own thick, hardened skin to perceive it. So, what I'm saying is, it's not all bad. She's the good part.

Comparing Alison Roman to storied baby boomer entertainer and cookbook writer Ina Garten, culture critic Alex Abad-Santos writes that Roman *is the realist inverse of Garten. She's a 34-year-old millennial living in Brooklyn whose home kitchen looks like it could maybe fit five people, standing shoulder to shoulder. But while Garten-like dinner parties for fabulous friends might not be Roman's reality, making food in a tiny space without a farmhouse sink or near-endless counter space is more relatable.*

Ina Garten never makes a joke at someone else's expense, and though she sometimes talks very quickly, especially in early episodes of her twenty years of food television, she doesn't ever say anything a reasonable person would want to take back. Is Alison Roman's acerbic wit and constant dishing against both friends and enemies her real personality, or is it just a television one? To me, these two women serve a similar function in my early postpartum depression. Sure, their kitchens are different, they're from different generations. But they are beautiful women making beautiful food beyond anything I could dream to make right now, and they have no children.

Like Garten, Alison Roman has something of a uniform: high-waisted jeans, well-fitting T-shirts, bright lipstick, hair tightly pulled back. Roman dropped out of college at nineteen to work in kitchens. Before she left school, she had been studying creative writing.

I want to look as effortlessly put together as Roman does. I know I look like something terrible has happened to me, and I don't like the way I look. I'm so soft, I feel like I've melted. Like with any ice cream cone, it is happening unevenly. When my children eat ice cream, I still sometimes need to take the reins, to grab the cone and lick around in a circle to even things out. When you look at me today, you can see the shape of what I once was, what once brought others some measure of joy.

There are a lot of things in Alison Roman's oeuvre that are, quite simply, not practical for feeding children. For example, she has an entire chapter in *Dining In* dedicated to what she calls *knife and fork salads*, dishes that, to me, sound destined to involve lots of knife screeching and items falling off the sides of plates, breadcrumbs and dressing flecks literally everywhere. Of course, there are the things in the book my children love: slow-roasted pork shoulder, chicken legs slow cooked in an unbelievable amount of fat. But if I wanted to observe someone useful, practical for my life of harried parenting, I would turn to Deb Perelman or to Ree Drummond. It turns out that what I want right now is to think about, to look at, someone beautiful. It's not that those other women aren't, it's just that they are in a way that feels like it belongs to the world that is trapping me. They're beautiful moms. I want to watch someone cook for friends who've never changed a diaper. Anna's face crumples in gentle concern. After many conversations with me, she is afraid of me and what I will do to myself. She keeps buying more bagels and cookies and doughnuts to placate me.

On her video series *Home Movies with Alison Roman*, Roman hasn't tried to reinvent herself after controversy. She's just leaned in harder to the same thing she was doing before.

There are the people it makes me sick to see, to watch, after learning about what they are really like. There are the obvious, the rapists and child abusers, the athletes who kill their wives. And then there are the more complicated cases, often white women I love to watch who fail to live up to what I want a public figure to be and do. Alison Roman is someone I feel drawn back to in the weeks and months I am floundering after birth. The other is Ellen DeGeneres. *Ellen DeGeneres: Here and Now*, a 2003 stand-up special in which the comedian tells an extended joke about being distractible, prone to procrastination, may have been one of the most important pieces of culture to me as a teenager. In the special, Ellen wears black slacks and a long-sleeve navy Henley shirt. She isn't feminine, but she isn't like the butch women I'd known in passing or on television, denimed and bandannaed and scowling. My sixth-grade teacher arrived to school each morning on her motorcycle, her hair in a close-cropped Afro, her affect impenetrably tough. Ellen smiles a lot, with big, bright teeth. She doesn't wear makeup, but she does wear earrings and some sort of a pendant necklace, not feminine, but still there.

When the special came out, when I was fifteen or sixteen, that was the height of my using food to punish myself, when I lived in a dreadful cycle of endless denial, when weight melted off me but it soon became clear that no matter how much I lost, I would never feel better. There was, however, a clarity of purpose in the morbid, narcissistic self-starvation: when denying myself food, I found I could focus on something like never before. Although, of course I knew then and know more sharply now that there is no benefit to anyone, least of all me, of having absolute laser focus on a coveted sandwich I will not allow myself to eat.

Roman has built a career on being someone who can get a party going. In this postpartum time, friends come to see me one at a time. They bring me foods, they're in control. They don't congregate, so it's not quite entertaining I do from the seated, breastfeeding position. My friends don't really even know one another, mostly, and it's hard to bring more people into a house that is already so full of people, so full that most nights feel like a dinner party, only not a good one, sometimes more like the dinner parties in novels, the ones that elicit *Hard Truths* or where things *Finally Come to a Head.* But do kids change you that much? Sure, Anna and I occasionally went to, even threw, parties, but we mostly socialized with one other person at a time. There was one friend, in our first apartment building, Anna's best friend from college, who would come over for dinner and would return the favor, who liked the same things I liked, stews and complicated French dishes—she was in a French literature PhD program—and with whom I shared warm conversation. And there was another friend of Anna's, who came over to complain to me about the high school where she taught, and then I'd return the favor and talk her ear off about mine. She worked at a school that had moved to a shiny new building across the street. *And the rats came with*, she said, dragging a piece of bread through some pasta sauce. And there was the friend who, half jokingly, referred to herself as my *adult practice child*, who would also come to my house to eat my food and complain about teaching. I have never been the life of any party, have never been even low-key kinds of fun. But in the last few weeks, I've sunk to a new low, and I worry I'll never come back from it. Instead of dreaming of an Alison Roman–esque party, I'm dreaming of being together enough to bake a tray of cookies without having a nervous breakdown.

And aside from the party aspect, there's something to be said about my jealousy over Roman's style, or attitude, or the way style and attitude converge, the white starched oxfords, the bright lipstick, the messy hair that looks messy in a studied way, and how she smiles but it's at her private jokes—they could be interpreted even as mean smiles. Meanness could be said to be anger's outlet, and I find myself angry with no outlet, holding a baby, alone on my couch. Roman is the one celebrity, other than DeGeneres, that I can't quit even though there is a clear, present cruelty to them, a hardness, like a friend who always says a thing you secretly think but would never be brave enough to say aloud.

We know now that DeGeneres was cruel, even abusive, to some of her employees, and based on that, it's safe to say that she isn't the kindest person. But twenty years ago, her work met me in a dark place and her wide-eyed, open humor, and the way she was unapologetically gay shook me awake (from her opener: *With all of our differences, we all have one thing in common: we're all gay. Now, there are people out there who are going, "Do they think we're gay because we're here?! Do we look gay? I told you this would happen. We're not going to understand a word of this"*).

The special isn't particularly focused on DeGeneres's queerness, but there is a gay person telling jokes, mostly about inattentiveness, that transfixed me as a teen. Her propensity toward procrastination is the thread upon which she strings clean, observational humor. I can look at clips from the special and see immediately what it is about DeGeneres's look that captured me. She was, like me, some third thing, something I might have called boyish years ago, though that feels silly now, a way of turning away from the responsibility I have to myself and the world I move through as a nearly-forty-year-old white man and father of four. She wore sneakers every day and looked best in clothes that were not exactly made for men but rather were tailored for a woman's body and made to look like they were for something else.

I'm not the only person of my generation who saw the possibility of a future life in DeGeneres. On the occasion of DeGeneres receiving the Carol Burnett award at the 2020 Golden Globes, Kate McKinnon becomes tearful as she shares, *In 1997 when Ellen's sitcom was at the height of its popularity, I was in my mother's basement lifting weights in front of the mirror and thinking, Am I gay? And I was. And I still am. But that's a very scary thing to suddenly know about yourself. It's sort of like doing 23andMe and discovering that you have alien DNA. And the only thing that made it less scary was seeing Ellen on TV.*

Mere weeks after McKinnon's speech, comedian Kevin T. Porter offered to donate two dollars to Los Angeles Regional Food Bank for every story posters told about Ellen's meanness.

Stories poured in.

I *believe that someday*, Ellen says in the special I loved in my earliest dark years, *sitcoms will be thirty seconds long, because that's all we'll need and that's all our attention span can take because our attention span is shot, we've all got attention deficit disorder, or ADD, or OCD, or one of the disorders with three letters because we don't have the time or patience to pronounce the entire disorder.*

Twenty years later, Ellen DeGeneres has revived her career, or tried to, in a comedy special on Netflix. We all know how these things go. She is mercurial, monologuing about her cancellation despite the platform she's literally standing on. The jokes are bitter. *Everybody heard that I was mean*, she says. *Everywhere I'd go, I'd know that everyone's heard that I'm mean.* But what interests me is the way she straightforwardly admits that's what her 2020 scandal pushed her to do: get evaluated. Twenty years ago, she described my life to me and told me that it was part of being in contemporary society to feel the way I do. Now, she says, she recognizes there was something else there.

I don't feel sorry for her, like I don't feel sorry for Roman, though I am sorry for myself, in a way, since I have little of the power and little of the wealth they have. But I do feel pangs of recognition in the ways we loop around what we're trying to say, how we go decades saying something to the side of it.

In a 2018 magazine profile, DeGeneres talks about how she never thought she'd grow up and have to be an adult. *I just didn't think I'd be alive*, she said, vaguely.

I know the night after the baby is born that things are not okay. I stay up late watching the Phillies lose the World Series. It happens like that, one minute there's hope and the next, we've lost. We had long believed that if we had a television in our room, that would mean giving up on hot sex, but Anna has moved one in for now so that something can keep me company, while I'm newly postpartum, while she takes over doing everything for everyone else.

There is a picture of Anna a day after we brought home our older daughter from the birth center. Anna is holding that baby, who has not been a baby for years now, her little head smushed perfectly in the crook of one elbow. Anna's shirt is pulled up because she is nursing. In the other hand, Anna is holding a fresh chocolate chip cookie. She's wearing floral leggings. The boys are sitting on the couch next to her, holding their own cookies. There are blankets and pillows everywhere. Anna is looking down at our daughter and smiling. It's a stupidly serene thing, this photograph, but the thing is, it really did feel like that. So peaceful, like we were finally good enough at the whole new-baby thing. Anna came home with our third kid happy and tired in a breezy sort of a way. I bought her a stack of trashy magazines and a big water bottle and brought up a basket of snacks and I played all day with the boys. I had taken four unpaid weeks off work and that time was a relief, as much as going slightly broke can be. The babysitter was canceled. I sat with the boys at breakfast and I sat with them at lunch. They both still needed booster seats. While the younger son took his three-hour midday nap, the older one spent an hour and half in his room, having what we called *Quiet Time*. Whatever he did in there, it wasn't my business as long as he didn't open the door. And the days, they moved. I didn't feel then like I do now: like every day lasts forever. Anna still says of her second birth, *I would give birth to that kid any day*. The third kid felt like just another step up in the chaos that had already been happening steadily for years. I met the challenge. And let's be real, I was still in my twenties, so young and full of life. A young back, young knees. It's only been a day but I know as I watch the Phillies lose to the Astros, the culmination of weeks of watching them in a miraculous-turned-shitty postseason, that some sort of doom is settling in this room, on me.

The moment I let my body descend from sitting to lying flat in the dark, I feel stunned, a wave of anxiety pulling me under. I am here now but I am also here last night while I screamed again and again as my placenta fell apart in pieces inside me and the midwife tried to remove it. The memory is not yet a memory; in a way, it feels like it is still happening to me every time I lie back. Memory is like that for me, layered like too many blankets on a bed. It's all happening simultaneously. There is a profound hurt that I feel all over my body. The center is where the baby came out of me, of course, but the pain radiates down my legs, up and around my back. It's the closest thing I've felt to Sunday-morning soreness after a Saturday rugby game, after being tackled and tackled and tackled again, held up by women much bigger and stronger than me. What happened here in this bed was bigger and stronger than me. The biggest tackle. The way Anna has anchored the baby's crib to the side of our bed frame makes it both a part of and apart from the bed. She sleeps on the side closer to the baby, telling me that

I need rest. Because she did not birth the baby, her body is not swirling with hormones and she's just regular dog-tired. Within seconds of lying down, she is asleep. I spend the next two hours in and out of sleep, in a haze, the porousness of states of awakeness dawning on me as I fail to ever reach a world in which I could dream, despite also not having slept last night. Then suddenly I'm in a state of being fully awake when the baby cries out for me, cries out to nurse, but I look at Anna, at the massive lump of her between me and the baby, and I look at the route I would need to take out of the bed on my side and around it to reach our new kid, who is still curled up and stiff, like an armadillo, just as she was inside me less than twenty-four hours ago, and I register the searing pain between my legs, in my back, in every muscle in my body, really, and I cry, abjectly, pathetically, maybe like never before in my life. I start quietly, but get louder and louder, until Anna jolts awake, somebody crying loudly on each side of her. There are times when I can't tell if I was trying to get attention or trying to avoid it. This is one of those. *What's wrong?* she says. *I just can't get to the baby*, I say. *Oh, honey*, she says, and hands me the eight pounds, four ounces of daughter I wanted so badly, so badly I'm worried I'll never be able to fully communicate it. The baby is at my breast again, and I am trying to coax my nipple into her new, confused mouth. My nipples are big and pink. I've been here before, and I know all the tricks, how to hold my boob like a sandwich, how to jam her little head on at just the right moment, but the baby and feeding her is not the problem. I am the problem. What is wrong with me? I am so tired but I can't sleep, I drift off but I'm still, a part of me is still so very awake.

It happens two hours later and two hours after that. One night can go on forever this way. I wake just as a panic attack is beginning. I haven't had one in years. How can a leap forward in time, baby in arms, also feel like a leap back?

There is also the other memory that lives alongside the trauma of the retained placenta and of the nights of painful half sleep that followed. It's of the moment my daughter emerged, into the midwife's arms. Anna was holding me half standing and I felt so safe, with the trans midwife and their trans midwife-in-training birth assistant and the photographer who was also a doula and Anna's friend the midwife, who sat with the older kids in the hallway for the long minutes before the baby's birth was imminent. Before the bad memories begin, there is the good one, a single thought: *I did it.* It's not fair that that moment, that day, was taken from me. And is it the biggest thing in the world? No. But I'm angry that the good parts don't win, cannot topple the pain. The memories of making soft-scrambled eggs with chives in the morning, of drinking an iced vanilla latte while walking around to get things moving, of rewatching *Homeland* with Anna in bed. *I think this labor is becoming a little too chill!* she'd cheerily said after the first episode ended, urging me out of bed. The last thing we did before we came upstairs to the bedroom was play Scrabble, standing in the kitchen, me in my underwear. And I won.

Our son has a plantar wart on his foot that will not go away. First we stuck the little bandages on it for him, and then we asked that he take over the responsibility, since we have other things to think about and do in the evenings. He's old enough to clip his own nails, to walk to local playgrounds on his own, so, we reason, he can stick a bandage on a wart. But the stubborn thing has persisted, and when he walks more than a block or two, he does it with a little limp whose existence he denies. Or he says he's sore from soccer practice. Or there's something wrong with his sock. But it's the wart, we think. So Anna texts her friend who is an emergency room physician and, as Anna says, reasonable prepper.

The doctor owns things we do not: land and a tricked-out bus you could live in for a while and a cellar stocked with food and basic necessities. The doctor says that to treat the wart we should crush aspirin into a paste with a little bit of water, put it on the wart, and cover the wart with duct tape. We have a mortar and pestle, one that I usually use to crush Szechuan peppercorns or cumin seeds or peanuts, and we have some other small bowls we could use besides. We settle on a little porcelain eggcup. Anna goes to Target to get the tape and the aspirin. *Promise me*, she says, after dinner, out of earshot of the kids, *that you won't try to kill yourself with it.* I shake my head. I have never tried but I think about it all the time, sometimes a lot for a few days or weeks, sometimes randomly once a month, sometimes not for a while, but it always creeps back. The years of the pandemic have been the longest and hardest struggle I've known. And recently it's been more than I can say out loud, more than I have told anyone. There are times it follows me, ruins me to think of, how my family would be without me, how they would always be people who had lost someone this way, and then there are times when I have to admit it soothes me, to think that this can't go on forever, my brain and self.

For the months after the baby is born, my mind always goes to the window: when I am done feeding and holding her and she is back asleep but still I am awake, I think of the relief of jumping out—the chilled air, gravity. The problem is, I know I might not die. Our home in Philadelphia is a row home, but only three floors, far from the thirty-eight feet of maximum height allowable by code, and in the end, if I jumped, I very well might live. Years before I met her, Anna's brother jumped off the roof of a campus building, during the brief period in which he was enrolled at a university, and survived, and though he died a few years after, and though I never met him, I have been haunted for years by the vision of his feet hitting the ground first, as I've heard happened. The heels, the legs, shattering.

When our son, the son with the wart, was young, we noticed how gifted he was at climbing trees. He could scale up trunks with no visible hand- or footholds, could balance on the thinnest branches. Sometimes other children tried to follow him, but mostly they could not even get into the tree without boosting one another. A memory: trying to get him to leave the wooden playground on Lake Superior's southern shore, when we lived blocks from it, rounding up his brother and sister and realizing I didn't know where he was. *Stay away from the water*, I would say, when I parked, again when I unleashed the three children inside the playground, fearing the lake, as was reasonable, above all other things in their lives. The moment I lost sight of one of them, I looked to the lake. Our son was so little, and it was hard to imagine he would in a short number of years be like the teenagers who jumped off the docks beside the park and into the water to go swimming, not a parent in sight. But my son was not in the water, he was in a tree, obscured by its branches, a blur of hoodie and Velcroed sneaker, a tiny voice getting tinier as he went up and up, shouting words I could not make out. *Come down!* I yelled, both wanting to look to make sure he did not fall and wanting to look away because I did not want to watch him if he did. He came down safely, an animal so skilled at movement. That night, I showed Anna a picture of our son in the tree, which I took the moment he began to descend. This haunting image of an arbor smudge prompted her to return to the emergency room where she worked to ask physicians how high he would have to climb to risk serious injury. My picture was proof of the danger. She says the physicians assured her.

Pushing the aspirin to the side of the counter, I cook the Polish dinner I make once a year to celebrate Anna's immigration to the United States in 1995, stuffed cabbage with sweet-and-sour tomato sauce, dozens of homemade pierogi with caramelized onions. I take pictures: of the pint-size mason jar I used to punch out dough circles, of rows of cutout circles topped with dense potato-and-cheese filling, waiting to be folded, one by one, by my so-very-much-living hands. As I taste the sauce, which is sharp and sugary, I know already that our children will not much like it. I have no special power to understand their thoughts, their feelings, their longings and fears, but there are times I feel like I am so attuned to their palates that we are closer to together than separate, as far as people go.

The dinner is good by virtue of the effort I put into it. A special celebration dinner. Anna is here, and because she is here, because she is no longer in Warsaw, we are here together. Anna says to me, when the children have left the table and she has asked me not to take the aspirin myself, that she tries *not to bring anything into the house you could use*. We do not have guns and neither of us takes any dangerous medications. But, we both know, of course, that I could hurt myself many ways, most notably with our car, which is dangerous at baseline and only increasingly so the worse I feel. *I would only do a boy suicide*, I joke, a hateful thing I say to end the conversation about pills, implying that I would hang myself, use a gun, do something violent that I could not survive. She walks away shaking her head. She does not repeat what she has said at other times: to put it in my own words, that it would ruin everyone but me.

When I was in graduate school, there was a morning when I said I was going out to write, when I dropped my sons off at the elementary school and my daughter off at her preschool and went to the library on campus and opened the program on the desktop and closed it and wandered through the stacks and picked up an issue of *National Geographic* and read, enraptured, a long profile of a young woman who as a teenager had shot off her face with a hunting rifle and then received a face transplant, performed at the Cleveland Clinic. She was, at twenty-one, the youngest person to undergo such a procedure. There were pictures. I reached out to touch them. In one, a group of doctors, gowned and gloved up, stand around a table on which a face is laid out flat, like a piece of fabric waiting to be sewn into a quilt. So many things ran through my mind, but the biggest two things were, first, how, like I'm talking step-by-step procedures, did she stop feeling the way she did the moment before, and second, why would she want the world to know what had happened to her, to see what had happened to her?

What I remember most about the article is realizing that teenagers are impulsive, and that is why they are especially in danger. In the video of the young woman speaking about her experiences, there is a slide stressing that impulsiveness is a key factor when teens die by suicide. But I'm impulsive, I thought, when I read it at thirty or thirty-one, I think again when I reread at thirty-six. The first times I really considered it closely followed the acquisition of my driver's license. I was queer in a small town both close to and impossibly far from a major city and I didn't see a way to have any kind of life I would want. Driving, to me, was beautiful. It made the town where I lived, the nearby night-black towns where my friends from the girls' parochial school we attended together lived, serene instead of oppressive, starry quiet. What struck me when I got behind the wheel was the freedom of driving, how I could go anywhere and my parents wouldn't know where I was. I didn't have a cell phone, and if I said I was going to a friend's house, well, they had six children and wouldn't have any way to contact anyone on the list of names I offered up, and did they even know who some of those people were? I took every long way, windows down, listening to pop rock full of young-boy despair and simple chords. It was the only time I sang. I loved the driving more than wherever I was headed, and one night it hit me: What if I ended it here, where I'm happy for once? No one relied on me to exist then, I cooked dinner for no one, and every time I've thought about it since I started dating Anna, it was heavier, not to mention the way that over the years I've come to realize how many people would be hurt by me: whoever pried me out of my car, whoever pronounced me dead, even if I managed not to wipe out any other cars, any pedestrians or construction workers.

Years later, here I am writing about what has happened to me: I wanted to die and it stopped and then I wanted it again and it stopped and then I wanted it again and when it was time to treat my son's wart, my wife, who has known me since soon after it started, brought home a bottle of aspirin and placed it smack dab in the middle of the counter where I cook our every meal and made me promise to grind it into a little paste to put on the wart and not to take it to try to end this life. The woman who received the face transplant did not die, but imagine all the people she traumatized by trying to. Everyone in the picture in which her new face lies waiting on a table is wearing a surgical mask. Even after these plague years, I can't read their expressions. But part of it must be horror, right? I didn't ask to be in this world and I don't want my absence to leave a hole in it, but it will, when it happens. When somebody in my house is hungry, I must feed them. When one of my children is hurt, Anna reminds me, I must care for them.

Looking at the arc of Roman's career is watching someone ascend, crash, coast, and crash some more. Escaping into the world of people who perform public lives that are widely scorned but many steps from what I'd consider horrifying is a comfort in the days and weeks and months I spend sliding back into a depression most mirrored in my teenage years. I am messing up right now, letting emails with opportunities go unanswered, losing touch with friends, alienating Anna and my older kids, and I want to watch others who have messed up.

I am running alongside the Delaware River listening to a profile of Alison Roman. I am a few months postpartum and I am in pelvic floor therapy to repair the damage that pregnancy and birth have done to my body. It's spring and I'm determined to run a half marathon before the baby turns one, because that is something I can will into happening. This fight, to move away from physical pain, allows a way for me to talk about recovery without telling people how depressed I am. I define *asynclitic* and describe the way my daughter's head tilted to the left until a few days before she was born, until I spent an afternoon slowly doing the Miles Circuit on our narrow staircase, walking and squatting and tilting through the house. I tell acquaintances about the retained placenta, but I don't go into detail, just remind them that I was at home, and so I had no option for pain management. *That's why running has been hard, but it's getting better*, I say, shaping my story into a triumph of sorts. I run by the casino and the arcade and on cobblestones through Old City. I run back to the water and head north, things becoming more and more industrial. Every time I leave, I wonder how I'll convince myself to run back to my baby and my life.

Lauren Collins's 2021 profile of Roman is titled "Alison Roman Just Can't Help Herself." To me, the thing that Roman can't stop doing is talking. She's quoted as much as a profiler can possibly quote their subject. In the first few months after a scandal caused much of the internet—and me, and the office mate who'd introduced me to her recipes—to balk at her lack of acknowledgment of her whiteness and how it emboldened her to publicly trash women of color whose marketing strategies she scorned, Roman was quiet. She started a newsletter and hinted at contrition. Collins writes, *Within a few months, though, one could detect hints of her old pugnaciousness intermingling with newfound caution.* When she talks to Collins or to other journalists Collins quotes, Roman is variously dismissive and combative, digging in her heels, especially when it comes to her responsibility as a white woman to credit the people and countries from which the dishes she riffs on originate. Collins writes: *As the writer Andrea Nguyen has observed, the brash, prescriptive "bro tone" that has served many a male food-world personality so well is increasingly becoming gender-neutral.*

It's so simple, the idea that you can do a basic weeknight chicken confit–like dish, cooking the chicken legs slowly in olive oil with vegetables. In the video, the moment she removes the chicken from the oven, it's one of the most iconic domestic images I can think of. I don't usually watch videos like this, weeknight chicken videos, because I have absorbed into every cell of my being a thousand ways to make a chicken. But I can't stop watching. I have watched each woman who cooks savory food on television or on the internet's version of personally branded television perform this action, touch chicken parts, talk about the skin, slice the lemon, choose an herb of the day. I perform these actions at least once a week and I know I will for the rest of my life, as long as that is. *It's extremely hot*, Roman says, *as you can tell by the cauldron-esque bubbles going on inside*. She's in denim and white. In the video, it's 2019, before everything. I had just started at the hospital and Alison Roman is at the height of her powers. On my tour of the hospital, I scanned my new ID again and again, entering and exiting corridors and lobbies, imagining I might work there forever. Roman is ascending, hoping for more books, for a television show, for fuss-free eternal stardom.

Collins writes, *When I met Roman, this fall, she compared the experience to that of a lobster in a pot of cold water. "You bring it up to a boil, they never know," she said. "And then they're dead."*

If my own temperature is ascending, if there is no sense that I know how to stop it, what will I do? How can I turn this around, turn the water off?

To start, I give the baby things she can hold on to: a huge hunk of a cucumber or carrot, a thick slice of avocado, half a banana. She seems betrayed by the taste of it, that it has a taste at all. She licks the banana and then puts her whole fist into it, liquefying it across the high-chair tray. For Anna's birthday, I agree to her one wish, to go away as a family to a state park cabin, though I don't want to. When will I look forward to things again? My days are a haze of stroller walks and dinners. If being a good partner is showing up even when you don't feel like it, I am doing a shitty job. I haven't even bought her a birthday card. The car ride is only an hour but I am losing my mind by the end trying to find this godforsaken cabin. I am watching myself and I want to grab my shoulders and shake: it's her birthday, you selfish ass. It's been 170 days since, Anna tells me, given my gaps in memory, she had to hold me down, *sit on you* is the phrase she uses, so that the midwife could reach inside me to remove my baby's placenta, the pieces of it that had broken away from the cord. I didn't even know they could do all that. Everything was going the way it should, and then I remember being told to push my placenta out, which should be easy and painless, and feeling nothing, no sensation, nothing coming, and there was a rush to lie me back down, and a quiet gasp around the room as everyone saw the cord come off with no placenta, and I was being told that it was going to be painful and difficult, and my children were rushed out of the room where they had all been admiring their wet, new, perfect sister, and I was screaming. What I remember saying between attempts to get the pieces out of me: *I'm sorry. I want you to do this. I'm trying to cooperate.* Always this deep desire to be seen as cooperating with anything that is happening, no matter how I feel. And then, *Am*

I going to be okay? And hours later, still in my bed, where all this had occurred, eating a pumpkin cake doughnut, trying not to get crumbs on the baby's head. A selfie of us, her mummified by blankets and a little baby hat, me bleary-eyed from lack of sleep. A picture of the doughnut, so pristine in my soft white hand, burnished with granulated sugar and flecks of ground cinnamon. Even in my depressed state, I have to admit the cabin is more than I expected. It is raining thunderously when we arrive and I prepare chili in the kitchen while the baby rolls around on the floor and Anna and the kids play cards, the chili ingredients chopped at home and preportioned into little eight- and sixteen- and thirty-two-ounce plastic tubs like I am on a cooking show. All I have to do now is stand and dump and stir. The chili is good and the pistachio cake I wrapped tightly in foil and more foil is good and I resist asking Anna if she is having a good time turning thirty-nine in the woods in a rainstorm with her wet dog and her four children and her miserable husband.

Ree

Nearly twenty years after I first discover Ree Drummond, I sit naked in bed nursing my daughter, one hand holding my phone over her head, the other holding a burp cloth to catch leaking milk. I watch again and again the video in which Drummond cleans out her pantry. Materially, I have it pretty good. We own a home and have a dual-income, middle-class family. There is nothing I truly want for in life.

And yet. This walk-in space, the wall-to-wall shelving, the granite countertops inside the pantry itself. More than any of that, I want to have the disposable income to purchase all those beautiful containers for the flours, the sugars, the pastas, the chocolate chips. Handfuls and handfuls of pecans filling one. The giant jars are spotlessly clean and each has a lid that fits. The sound of lids being taken off containers. Pop. Snap. Pop. She nests vintage Pyrex bowls. She lifts multiple dutch ovens up onto a shelf. None of her baking dishes are scratched. Clink clink clink, she lines up a dozen bottles of Topo Chico. She has not one but two boxes of Droste cocoa powder. I want to live in this pantry.

For Autostraddle's 2017 *Queer in the Kitchen* series, over two hundred queers sent in captioned photos of their kitchens. Some photos contain no people, some have one person, a few feature a couple. There are significantly more pets than children. Curiously, three of the respondents are naked in their photos, turning their kitchens into spaces that could be read as erotic, or otherwise as spaces of complete privacy, where you don't even need to throw on a robe to go pour yourself a glass of orange juice. And in this sense, privacy comes to mean freedom.

None of the kitchens are opulent, though some have that renovated apartment look: stainless steel, subway tile, sleek countertop. Others are very spare, there's maybe a boxful of belongings, all told. Some of captions are too short, don't satisfy my curiosity. Did you install that shelf yourself, or was it there when you moved in? Can you open the pantry and give me a peek? I look around my own kitchen: dozens of plates, a cabinetful of mugs, appliances taking up every centimeter of space. Shelving and more shelving, a magnetic strip of knives. A twenty-five-pound bag of rice atop a high cabinet, sacks of flour and sugar, cans of oats, everything looking like it once had a place but was put back in another one. No matter how many times my family moves, we never pare the kitchen down.

I imagine myself cooking for the rest of my life in every kitchen I see. In friends' kitchens, I think about the distance between the countertop and the stove, I think about how our dishes would fit in the dishwasher, I imagine cleaning the backsplash, or installing a new one. In my imagination, I sweep errant cat food off the floor and pull gunk out of the sink drains. Most of the kitchens I have known belonged to straight people. I've rarely been inside another trans person's kitchen.

In my favorite photo from the series, Megan, a twenty-three-year-old white, butch-looking horticultural therapist living in Hawaii, stands in the dirtiest kitchen in the series. They hold a mug and wear a ball cap. They look to the side. Their caption reads, *I woke up super early this morning and couldn't fall back asleep, so I walked into the kitchen and just started cooking things. I ended up with a pumpkin curry soup, cinnamon toasted pumpkin seeds, and some avocado pesto. Some people get lost in playing music or painting or doing photography; I cook.*

On her television show *The Pioneer Woman*, which has gone on for thirty-eight seasons, Ree Drummond cooks in a huge but homey-looking kitchen. There's a beautiful stone archway around a window, which looks out onto vast land. You see the land in many of the shots, shots of fields, shots of cows, shots of children or cowboys riding horses. In season 1, episode 1, Drummond cooks chicken-fried steak. *Out here on the ranch*, she starts as she puts cube steak into seasoned flour, *the guys have been working so hard*, getting up at five in the morning each day, and that is why they need to eat something that *sticks to their ribs*. She dredges the steak into egg, which gums up in a yellowish egg-flour sludge on her fingertips.

Out here, Drummond says, referring to all that land. If it looks endless through that kitchen window, or when the camera pans back and captures her husband and other men riding horses in waxed jackets, that's because, essentially, the land *is* endless. As of 2017, the Drummonds, based in Osage County, Oklahoma, were the twenty-third-largest landholders in the United States, with a total acreage over four hundred thousand.

Ree Drummond cooks like a home cook. While making gravy, she pours milk directly from a red-topped gallon jug into a hot pan. To remove the pan-fried steaks from her cast-iron skillet, she sticks a fork in each one and lifts it onto a paper towel–lined baking sheet, the way my mother would.

Between close-up shots of meat in a skillet, four white children chase a soccer ball up a rolling hill in their jeans, chambray shirts, and cowboy hats and boots.

On another early episode, Drummond cooks steak sandwiches for two. The sandwiches aren't the same, though; on some of her episodes, Drummond cooks his-and-hers versions of the same food. Her husband, Ladd, is a *real meat and potatoes guy*, she says, so it may freak him out if he's faced with any of the vegetables she's going to put on her own sandwich. *Arugula*, she says with wide eyes, as if it's a green that arrived in rural Oklahoma from another planet.

Ladd wears utility gloves when he pulls up in his truck, even though he's not going to carry any tools. Instead, he lugs a basset hound out of his dusty Ford F-150 and heads inside for a sandwich.

The show's style deemphasizes the vastness of the kitchen and the ample pristine shelving, thousands upon thousands of dollars of items, ceramic vessels and bowls and more that Drummond may or may not reach for on a regular basis. There's a massive enameled farmhouse sink, fresh flowers in a vase beside it. Instead of sticking with these things, the camera cleaves closely to her hands and to the cast-iron skillet, the cutting board, where she runs a knife through meat for her husband. I'm watching someone cook, but not learning much. I learn seeing how a cook lines up what they need, how many bowls they have out, how they move. My eyes are forced to look into Ree's in unsettlingly intimate close-ups. But I look around any chance I get. Rewatching early episodes, I assume that she films in her own kitchen, but then I learn that while she owns this kitchen, it's not inside her residence, but rather at the Lodge, which is a guesthouse on her family's property.

It's 2023 and I'm a stay-at-home parent for the second time. Years ago, I stayed home with our sons for one school year. I was excellent at the work of staying at home, at carrying two babies around at once, at filling our days, at robotically filing away baby books and toy trains when they went to bed, knowing I would do it all again the next day. I don't regret how I spent that year, but I didn't love it, and so this isn't something I've longed for. Once again, it seems to make sense for a while, for me to be childcare, and I plan to go back to teaching next September, when the baby's close to one.

She doesn't like to be put down, not in a swing, not in a bouncy chair, not in a bassinet or in a stroller, just like our other children at her age. She sleeps against me in a baby carrier, while I walk around the neighborhood, which is dense and full of people and stores and exhaust fumes and trash smell. Even in this hard city, people's faces soften a bit when they see my daughter. While my older children go to school, I am in one of two positions: upright, with the baby sweat-stuck to my chest, or sitting on the couch, airing out and scrolling on my phone.

On the internet, increasingly aestheticized at-home parenting is creeping in to my feed. I am, in a sideways sort of way, the target audience. These "momfluencers," as culture writer Sara Petersen terms them, have relentlessly clean countertops and make motherhood look fun and effortless. *I'm fascinated*, Petersen writes, *by the thousands of mothers on Instagram who make it look magical, like the only thing anyone would ever want to be.* Influencing isn't new, but the migration from the blogs of my early parenting days onto short video blasts makes it all feel more persistent and absorbing. I hate-watch women packing snacks, setting up crafts, going on hikes, things I do, things I mostly *like* to do. But there's a sinister, coercive nature to the content. With everyone smiling and nothing looking hard, it feels doable, desirable even, to build your entire world around the inside of your home.

Growing up, as my mother shoved plate after plate of sandwiches and snacks across the counter at us, I planned other kinds of life for myself—I didn't know I would end up a man, but I did know I didn't want this, this tether to chores. But here I am. When Anna and I started our family, we didn't talk about who would do what. But I could cook and she could not, and we fell into a rhythm centered around the meals I make. My own four young children seem to want lunch the moment I'm done cleaning up after breakfast. I have, in a way, become my mother, my family's pioneer woman.

Drummond's cultural celebrity began with a blog she launched in the aughts, on which she wrote about her daily life, including what she cooked for her husband, their four children (she and Ladd began parenting a fifth child, a teenage foster son, who is Black, when her other children were teens and young adults). The cheesy wholesomeness of her photographs and stories of homeschooling on the ranch and her cheeky jokes belied the vast cattle empire she married into. Her in-laws have been in Oklahoma since the late nineteenth century, around the time the Osage came there from Kansas.

Drummond has a particularly American pull, embedded in her name: even for white Americans like me and Anna, whose families came to the United States in recent generations and never left the East Coast, there may be, deep inside, a nostalgia for a simpler life in the violent wake of westward U.S. expansion. There's the more immediate nostalgia that I feel, too, for my mother's table. I probably gravitated toward Drummond's recipes first because they seemed like things I could cook for my parents and siblings, when I visited home, due to the volume and lack of "fussy" ingredients (Drummond lives far from a grocery store, as she emphasizes frequently, and her rich husband has the palate of a toddler).

When I'm home, with my family of origin, I eclipse my mother's role as the cook. The cook doesn't have to socialize as much, doesn't have to drink as much, can be a little weird, just as long as the dinner's good. The kitchen is a place to hide from the pressure, the banter. The unsettling feeling I got as I aged—that who I was in my own home and who I had been in the home in which I was raised were fundamentally incompatible—melts away when I am scooping out cookies onto one of my mother's baking trays. Maybe that's what drew me into the kitchen in the first place. The pressure's different—not on how you act but rather on what you make.

The Pioneer Woman cooks grilled chicken, burgers, one-pot pastas, those sort of things. In her world, meat is on the table daily, and potatoes pass as vegetables. It's not beautiful food, which is why she gravitated, in her early blogging years, toward photos of fields and hills, of cows and the men who herd them. Rather than beauty, the food serves another purpose: volume. More often than not, the recipes I want to try are portioned for two to four people, and I approach each one with a plan to double or triple what's written. Not with Ree.

When we were kids, my mother served us food like this: chicken cutlets at least twice a week, a giant meat loaf on a sheet pan, flank steak on a night she felt fancy, burgers on the grill when she didn't want to have too much cleaning to do. There's a nostalgia in that food, but as my siblings aged, more of us spent years or decades as vegetarians or vegans, or just didn't want to eat like that anymore, didn't want food to weigh us down. When I visit their apartments, I open their cabinets and find grains, beans, condiments. None of them have kids, so I imagine they haven't made grilled cheese or tossed a bag of fries in the oven in years.

It's hard to resist Drummond's dessert recipes, the kinds of unfussy desserts kids love: a massive Texas sheet cake baked on a half sheet pan, a peanut butter pie with Oreo crust, a puckeringly tart lemon icebox pie topped with whipped cream. Nothing requires a mixer or a visit to a specialty store.

Amanda Fortini quotes Bobby Flay in a 2011 profile of Drummond: *Her cooking strikes a chord with lots of people in this country who are interested in feeding their families better food without getting into molecular gastronomy.*

In her wide-ranging 2011 profile of Drummond, surmising about the Pioneer Woman's fame, Fortini writes of the choices Ree Drummond has made as literary choices: *The amateur country-girl persona works as a literary device because it allows readers to imagine falling in love and ditching their frenzied lives for a calmer, more agrarian existence, without having to abandon the notion that they are sophisticated, independent women.*

For me, it's a *She's like me, only she lives out there* sort of a thing. Parsing through Fortini's words, a friend and I—neither of us had children yet—were trying to determine how right-wing Drummond was, how much it was okay to like her, okay to watch her. Of course, she had all the hallmarks of someone I could not have in my life, not in a close way, anyway: church, homeschooling, all that land. Was she really something like us?

When I first found Drummond, her life did seem like something to aspire to. Living in Philadelphia, stepping over mounds of trash, needles and dirty diapers and take-out refuse, all just to get onto the subway, to get to the bus station, to get on the bus to work, who wouldn't want to live out in the country far from people? My life was so very peopled, by students and then by my own children too. As improbable as this life seemed for me, an unhappy twenty-something closeted trans man, wasn't it improbable for Ree also? That was the point: she was a woman who had left Oklahoma to attend the University of Southern California, and she became a city girl. She only ended up on a ranch because she met her husband in a bar while back home, temporarily, she thought, because of that improbable way love can reorient the trajectory of your life.

Lately, as I consider Ree Drummond, I can't stop thinking about Curtis Sittenfeld's short story "The Prairie Wife." In the story, Kirsten, a thirty- or forty-something working mom of two kids, cannot stop reading social media content created by Lucy Headrick, a woman with whom Kirsten had a fling the summer after her freshman year of college. In the twenty years since, Lucy has morphed from a self-declared college lesbian into a Ree Drummond–like figure: a Missouri proto-tradwife with 3.1 million followers.

Kirsten is married to Casey, a partner for whom Sittenfeld conveniently avoids using pronouns and words like *husband* and *wife* in describing. The first time, I admit, I thought Casey was a dude. I can't remember what I was doing while I listened to Sittenfeld read her story. Chores, probably. Listening to short stories while I scrub toilets and refill hand soaps from a big tub of clear Target-brand soap makes me feel literary, like I belong in the world of words. But how well can you absorb something in those conditions? As I cleaned, my mind filed away Casey as a husband. I guess I thought that Kirsten saw Lucy as some sort of road not taken because, in the story, Kirsten says, cruelly, that sex with Lucy isn't real sex. To her, sex with another woman is a warm-up act to better, realer sex she will have with men. For some reason, I believed that immature Kirsten of the flashback. That she married Casey, a man. But then, it's revealed—though is it a revelation to anyone but me?—that Kirsten ended up with a woman. In that way, the famous and unbelievably wealthy Lucy was not a warm-up but rather a gateway into a world of queerness.

But what sort of queerness? The story is about a boring domestic trap. One in which queer parents are negotiating who wakes the kids up, who makes breakfast, and who will bring the forgotten instrument to school. They're wondering what it means if your exhausted co-parent does or does not put their arm around you before sleep. It's unsettlingly unsexy and hard, something usually limited to the world of literature about cishet people. Kirsten and Casey are mostly too tired to have sex, and when Casey leaves for work, Kirsten masturbates in the shower thinking of Lucy Headrick. Is her life with Casey ever going to involve romance again? *This is what this stage is like*, Casey says to Kirsten near the end of the story, as they lie in bed together, knocked out by their days. Kirsten is worried about how time is passing, how they will look back at this part of their lives.

Anna and I, we had the opposite worry. Our daughter, our third child, turned five. She went to kindergarten. We let our older son walk his siblings to and from school. We left them at this playground, then this other one. We told babysitters, *You don't . . . honestly really need to do anything with them.* We hired a babysitter who was in nursing school and told the kids to leave her alone, to just let her study. They walked themselves to the corner store and to the doughnut shop. I watched them morph into Philadelphia pedestrians, not believing in the power of any light or stop sign. They would stand at the corner, crane their necks far into the street, step out one step, and wait to be waved on by the driver. They listened to news radio and science podcasts. They read big books and had real ideas. My time with very young children was passing. I was in my early thirties, then I was in my midthirties. And Anna and

I said, Wait, we need this to go on, we aren't done with this. Whatever this chaos is, this is where we need to be. And that is when we had our fourth.

Back when Anna and I were in college, we were going out to rent a movie when we had an argument, not for the first time, about how to be in the world as a unit: how to act around our parents, what it meant to be out, in which states we would hold hands. Who knows which topic the self-absorbed being-a-queer-kid-fucking-sucks spinning wheel landed on. But she said something that made me realize she was grieving the world of straightness, the world I never for a minute thought I would be a part of. I didn't have the words for it, but I was always set apart. Never, not once, did I picture myself in a wedding or a baby shower or on the other side of the table at a parent-teacher conference. In these moments, Anna would always remind me of the fake weddings adults orchestrated at the Polish scouting camp she attended as a little girl. She was little, in elementary school, and she was matched with some boy she barely knew. To be fake married at that age would have horrified me, but she loved it. She loved the dream of it all, loved the possibility of what her life would have been like. She dreamed of her wedding and of her babies. She cared lovingly for her doll. *But we can have that*, I told her. *Don't you see that? We can have the same things they have.*

The parallels between Lucy Headrick and real-life mom bloggers, who have sold readers and viewers on rigidly nostalgic, rural white motherhood for the last twenty years, are clear. Lucy has 3.1 million followers on Twitter; Ree Drummond has 4.4 million followers on Instagram. Watching Lucy bake in a television appearance makes Kirsten feel *such rage at Lucy that it was almost like lust.*

Drummond and Headrick, the real and the fictional, ironically achieve notoriety from digitizing domesticity, tasks that rely heavily on the body, tasks that can only be delegated into another's hands: feeding the chickens, pushing the mop. Headrick could easily be read as Ree Drummond, except that as readers, we have insight into Headrick's queer-inflected past. It would be a big deal for Kirsten to expose her, to out her, there's heat there. And the reason for the exposure wouldn't be moral clarity but rather pettiness; Kirsten would only do it because she's dissatisfied with her own life. For Kirsten, the two things Lucy holds, flirty lesbian camp counseling coworker and tradwife, cannot exist within the same person, and it's something burning a hole in her every day.

Where's the heat behind Ree Drummond? The universe of the Pioneer Woman is as straight as can be. Ladd wears tight Wranglers and works the land, while Ree stays inside making beef stew. You'd think a queer life would be a radical life, a moving away from what Ree and Ladd have. But as queer couplings have moved into the mainstream, the domestic angst once squarely within the purview of straights has become our sphere too.

To make a family was, just generations ago, radical in itself. Historian Sara Matthiesen writes, *Lesbians who became pregnant through artificial insemination beginning in the 1970s explicitly identified home, family, and reproduction as necessary sites of political transformation.* Lesbian family creation could throw a wrench in the existing capitalist landscape, with lesbian mothers applying for state benefits to support themselves in their children's infancy. This, according to Matthiesen, *prompted the state to go looking for the player so central to the privatization of dependency: Father.*

As wealthier, whiter lesbians figured out how to work within existing legal and medical systems, and to expand those systems to protect middle-class queer families, it became clear that, as Matthiesen writes, there was a *disciplining effect of being subsumed into the norm.* Being a queer family who'd used a legal marriage, a sperm bank, and the auspices of second-parent adoption made you, as you worked within the system of nuclear family codification, become a part of it.

There's something else with the Drummonds, though. Writing in *Vanity Fair*, film and television journalist Eve Batey connects the Drummond family to the violent white settler colonialism depicted in Martin Scorsese's *Killers of the Flower Moon*, an adaptation of David Grann's 2017 investigative journalism book of the same name. Each centers around corrupt cattleman William King Hale, a convicted murderer responsible for a complex land inheritance–related plot that resulted in the death of at least twenty Osage people, many of whom had acquired wealth after the discovery of oil on their land.

The Drummonds now own about 9 percent of the Osage County land once in Osage tribe control. The first Drummond in Oklahoma opened the Hominy Trading Company, once the nation's largest seller of Pendleton blankets, in the last decade of the nineteenth century. Overcharging for goods and services, making land grabs, their violence was a quieter, subtler version than Hale's.

Ruby Hansen Murray, an Osage essayist, writes about a visit back home to Oklahoma from the Bay Area. She visits The Pioneer Woman Mercantile, a restaurant and store Ree Drummond opened in the closest town to her ranch, Pawhuska.

Murray writes, *The conflation of ranch or farm families with wholesomeness, with whiteness, is potent. Some Americans want to believe this veneer is the only version of itself. America has a problem with memory and with the truth, with rationalization and with clear thinking, with complicity and expedience.*

Murray notes the scant references Drummond makes to the Osage, the silence that is another iteration of white violence. She confronts this lack of complication in light of her own complicated feelings about Oklahoma, as an Osage now living in the Bay Area. Murray's job, family, and desire to live away from the red-state politics keep her in a state of disconnect from Osage land. *No matter how many times I come home, I miss parties, powwows, book groups, hand games and celebrations, funerals, church meetings, and driving on the prairie.*

Seeing a white woman celebrating her life in the Osage, she writes, *is hard, because she does look happy.*

I think about my first time staying home with my boys, the deep loneliness I felt complaining about what amounted to the ultimate luxury: quitting your job and spending all day playing with your kids. They're thirteen months apart, and the thing I remember most about that year is pushing a stroller up and down Frankford Avenue, beginning at dawn, stepping off that long thoroughfare to hit up one park and another, the bagel shop, the play group. Anything not to have to go back home, where they would throw every toy on the ground and try to gouge each other's eyes out. One day, I stopped to get an iced tea with the boys. An acquaintance was there, having coffee with a woman I didn't know. They wore business-casual clothing and had laptops. *This is Krys, who makes it look easy*, the acquaintance said.

The Pioneer Woman Cooks: Food From My Frontier is in the pantheon of cookbooks my mother and I exchange back and forth, many of which had their origins as blogs or food television content, or both. I keep mine on a neat, uncluttered shelf in the kitchen, and she keeps hers behind a glass cabinet door, lined up in a row. I buy her books by the authors of blogs like *Smitten Kitchen* and *Homesick Texan*. She buys me nearly every title from the Barefoot Contessa universe. I know my mother will like many of Ree Drummond's recipes because they are pretty good, feed a crowd, and appeal to Ladd's palate, which is similar to my father's. My mother and I, we get along. Our relationship as adults, it's good. We FaceTime a few times a week, and she DMs me recipes from blogs around the internet. We both want to be eating fancy food, trying exciting new things, but instead, we're serving chili around a big table, passing a chip bag and fielding complaints over who gets what spoon.

We are in the same universe of content, though she's a conservative older woman, and I'm her kinda weird trans son. My internet is the mothers' internet, the same one Kirsten watches, the one Ree Drummond and Lucy Headrick create, the one Sara Petersen criticizes. The more children I have, the more the internet thinks I want my content to revolve around them. Over the years, I've noticed it shifting more and more toward telling me what I, as a presumably white and middle-class user of a phone, should feed my children.

First, there's breast milk, of course. Then there are the perfect foods, organic and lovingly prepared in a clean, spacious kitchen. They title their videos things like "What Three Months of Breastfeeding Did to My Baby," "What My Six-Month-Old Eats in a Day," "What My Twelve-Month-Old Eats in a Day." I view montages of homemade purees, children holding slippery avocado halves, a chef who makes his toddler professionally presented dishes on tiny white plates.

And though the internet I create is full of beautiful things, I'm the first to admit I bake swirled brownies and fresh sandwich bread because I have to, not because I'm better than anyone else. There is a thrumming need within me: to move my body, my hands, to make something of my time, to please the people I've helped bring into the world. To be and stay animated by my, and by others', cyclical hunger. It's how I relate to people, this creating. A photograph of a *Smitten Kitchen* peanut butter–filled chocolate cookie I post on Twitter is an invitation, not for anyone to tell me what a great parent I am but for people to tell me how fucking delicious it looks, to ask for the recipe, to tell me they made it too, to joke, *What work thing are you avoiding by making these?*

In a way, I am like the mothers of the internet, the mothers in my life, too, only I am not them, because I am not a mother. I perform many of the same actions: spraying countertops with that one spray that won't leave streaks, sharpening chef's knives, thinking of little hacks to make my life make sense to me. In their reels, the mothers make fun of their husbands, who are hapless and cannot grocery shop, cannot care for infants effectively, cannot understand them nor all the things they do. It's tiresome but I am shown this content for a reason, am I not? Why do I spend minutes at my desk watching a white woman in a clean-looking suburban kitchen put a rotisserie chicken in a large ziplock bag, massage the bag vigorously with both hands, and separate the meat from the bones in a warm, smeary mess? This is supposed to save me time. It's a hack. I am part of the target audience. I am making a dinner a cowboy would love. The only vegetable in it is an onion. There are two kinds of shredded cheese. My head is out the back door and I am calling everyone in for dinner.

My mother calls me one evening because she accidentally bought cauliflower gnocchi to make a sheet pan gnocchi recipe I sent her, chicken thighs, olive oil, garlic, dried seasonings, nary a vegetable, though I tell her you can put any cubed vegetable on the sheet pan to round it out, knowing she won't—and she wants to let me know she's just going to do it! She's going to throw the cauliflower gnocchi on the sheet pan like it's regular gnocchi and serve it to my father without telling him! He would never touch cauliflower knowingly. My mother is drunk on light beer she's drinking from a wine glass in her kitchen. She likes kitschy, hand-painted wine glasses. I don't see the beer or the glass but I know from her voice and the way her ears are burning red. *Mom, he's gonna know! He'll hate this dish forever!* I tell her. I'm sitting on the childish living room carpet, one with illustrated roads for toy cars, and I am giggling too. I call her a lot during transition times, when the baby wants to be doing something she can't be doing right then. These transition-time calls began when I was an undergraduate, not long before I met Anna, when I would want someone to keep me company as I traversed the entire green campus on my way to class. She would tell me what she had for lunch, what was on tonight's dinner roster.

My mother would make a terrible momfluencer. She has a beautiful home, a beautiful kitchen, and six beautiful children, but she has no filter, and she's a complainer. She's brash and judgmental and hilarious in a way that influencers, and food celebrities, are not. Ruby Hansen Murray writes of Ree Drummond, *I like Ree best when she is unscripted. I laughed when she posted a video of a rat running across the floor during a cooking show she was filming.* If my mother had a cooking program, it would likely be a lot of that.

My mother and I don't talk about hard things. Questions like does she think my life is turning out all right, is she proud of me, am I making some huge mistake raising my kids, but they're not worth giving too much thought, because I don't believe in asking questions I don't want to know the answers to.

The baby wants to be asleep, she is in her pajamas, but it isn't bedtime. It's six in the evening and I do not want to be awake at the hour she'll wake up if I let her sleep right now. The baby is tired. She points to her sleep sack, her pacifier, the staircase that leads to her bedroom. My mother tries to get the baby's attention. *Baby girl, say hi to Grandma! Take that pacifier out of your mouth!* The baby halfheartedly waves at my phone.

Anyway, my mother says, *I put the package in the trash can and covered it with other stuff. Fingers crossed.* We are similar, but I didn't marry someone like my father. Anna grew up in Poland eating so few things, because of scarcity, because her mother was not a skilled cook, but she will eat anything I put on the table. She loves leafy greens, kale and chard and arugula, an extra-sharp vinaigrette, salad with a split soft-boiled egg on top, the jars of chili crisp I keep all in a row in the fridge. She loves the snap of a green bean and simple steamed bok choy. *More for me*, she'll say, taking the vegetable dishes away from the kids and pulling them toward her plate at the corner of the table.

In two years, I will have been in this relationship longer than not. My sensibility about what to cook and what to eat is growing up along with hers. We have left our mothers' homes and grown up together in a city with an amazing food culture, and we have tried many things for the first time in one of the seven kitchens we have shared. We don't get out to eat much, but when we do, she lets me pick where to go, what to order. At home, too, I pick everything. I decide how to arrange and stock the refrigerator. I select the brands, and the family's tastes evolve with mine. Once I buy Kerrygold butter for our toast, I'm never going back. I like thighs better than breasts, so our chicken choices are done. My favorite apples in a bag. My favorite yogurt in a big quart container. When I ask if anyone has any cravings or desires, I get a resounding murmur of neutrality. It's such a trap, because that means I have to pick everything, but I don't know what it would be like, having to eat things someone else picked. That hasn't been my life since I was a kid. On nights that we finally go out after months of eating all our meals at home, Anna and I split everything, our hands tearing into it all. What's the point of picking, she wonders, when I always seem to choose what's best on the menu? Out of the house, out in the world, I stop feeling like somebody's housewife, which is often something I sink into. She laughs because I tell her the song "Where Have All the Cowboys Gone?" is really about me. *Because I make more money?* she says. *Because of . . . I don't know, everything!* I tell her. The way the woman in the song is hot for someone who goes out and makes money in a big, bodily way, hot for the way it feels to wait at home for it. Until it stops being hot. Because, maybe, I want to say to Anna, it would be nice if you noticed how much work it takes to keep the house functioning. I put the song on every playlist for months. She rolls her eyes whenever it comes on. What a mournful, dramatic little boy she lives with. Did I want to be the pioneer woman in the song, or am I mad that that's kind of just the way it went?

Anna's father was so upset when she went to nursing school, lost his mind at seeing her in a service profession. In Poland, she told me, nursing was more of a working-class job than it is here, though when she talks about what she likes, she emphasizes that the work is done with the hands, that it is done on the feet, that it involves touching the body, that it must be done at a quick and automatic pace in order to keep up with its demands. She talks about it the way I talk about making yet another vat of spaghetti for dinner. What did her father want? For her to be an economist, a mathematician, something fancy, I think. Something he perceived as clean. Some job where you never touch someone else's poop. And what if she did? Whenever the children are sick and we are hovering over their beds through the night, holding out one bowl and another for them to vomit into, she says, *No matter who you are, no matter where you went to school, you're just a body taking care of other bodies.*

The Pioneer Woman is good at taking pictures of her children, always has been. She doesn't share their rough moments, which I respect. It's not really her place, and it's also not really her thing. They are defined characters, with names, but they are also a pack, which can happen once you have more than one or two children. I do wonder if she takes pictures of her kids, some of whom are adults now, when they're under the weather or just being annoying, for herself. I have those pictures, of my children feverish and mummified by blankets, lying on the couch with ice pops hanging from their mouths. For me, there's something about admitting I spend a lot of my time thinking about other people's bodily functions, but also that it doesn't define any of us. We're all just people trying to make it through the day, but our days are bound up together. I don't know how the gnocchi went over. How, after decades upon decades of shopping to feed my father, lasers would not strike my mother as she reached out to touch a package of cauliflower. Why do we need to make cauliflower into everything, anyway? What I do know is that I made the sheet pan gnocchi at least once a week for months, because the idea of cooking everything together makes dinner seem less arduous. How can gnocchi out of a package get so good, so crispy, all coated in chicken fat and salt? What I did not say before is that a part of me is always hoping I'll find a recipe so regular slash fancy that it'll give me a reason to call my mother.

Ina

I'm not just depressed. There's something else, too, a way in which I'm not functioning the way I should, or could. I remember a friend who got accidentally pregnant and decided to keep the baby, despite not knowing if the relationship would last. She hadn't known if she wanted to mother, before she became pregnant, but soon after her son was born, she told me how well he slept early on, how easy he was, that if God only gave you what you could handle, he had known she couldn't handle much and had given her the baby to match.

What if the thing I wanted, this fourth baby, placed me beyond my capabilities? You can't know until you're in it, I guess, and now I'm in it. Three just felt so doable, and now there's been a sort of mental spilling over. I cannot hold four children in my head, cannot manage to get all of them to put their clothes on or leave a playground with me. One is always going missing or didn't hear me or forgot their water bottle on a bench that is the farthest away from where I need them to be. Sometimes I teach writing classes at night, on Zoom, sessions that last a month or two, and I start again when the baby is just a few weeks old, hoping to meet myself on the other side, that old me. I tell my writing students they will never know their limits until they pass them. *Do the most*, I say. Make an abundance of clay, then make something out of it. They will need first to write sentences that are too long, scenes with too much dialogue, essays that reveal too much. One of my own teachers referred to this sense of writing as *too much of a muchness*. It's stuck with me, that out-of-control phrase for an out-of-control feeling. I tell my students to go there, because they can always scale back. But it's the kind of advice that is so good for writing and so utterly terrible in most other circumstances. Is my fourth child the maximalist decision that will prove to be my too much?

Days Anna goes to work and the big kids go to school, there's a version of this life that would amount to living in a dream. There's not a future me that exists clearly, so who knows if it'll be teaching at a high school or an elementary school or somewhere else entirely in a year. For now, I'm staying at home with this perfect baby who smells faintly bready and milky, like something fresh that won't last long. I wash her daily with Johnson & Johnson soap. I want that timeless baby soap odor, the one I smelled when I washed my youngest sister, who was thirteen years younger, who also had blond hair and big blue eyes and who also felt so sturdy and real in my teenage hands, not fragile at all. Because they're not fragile, they're people who haven't been tested yet, they're resolute. This baby in my hands is living through my depression and through my feeling that there is another something I must confront to make it through.

On days home alone with her, you can find me sunken into our beaten tan couch watching early seasons of *Barefoot Contessa*, a television show that aired before I had this baby or the last, before I met Anna, before I went away to college. There's a timelessness to Ina Garten, both in appearance and style. It's as if she's holding strong for another generation of viewers. She does seem nervous in the first few episodes, as she talks quickly through wooden conversations with her own friends and shop owners she clearly knows well, but otherwise this first season could've been filmed yesterday. I pause my abject days of loneliness and overwhelm to watch Ina Garten go through seasons of her own fabulous days in the Hamptons.

Ina Garten's life is a magical escape.

My own current life is a swirl of parenting advice, pat sayings that form an ambient soundtrack to my stay-at-home dad life. It doesn't only come to me through the algorithm; strangers say these things to me in person when they see me and the baby passing by. Maybe I'm pointing out a pretty tree or a flower, or maybe she's screaming while I change her diaper at the park. *The years are short but the days are long* is a thing people say that feels deeply true, unlike *Enjoy every minute* or *One day, you'll miss this*. As a toddler, my second son sat in my lap, banana in hand, watching episodes of *Barefoot Contessa* when he could not sleep, though he doesn't remember a thing about any of this, the insomnia or the way Ina Garten lit up our living room television screen. He loved watching her shop, loved the flower arrangements she set out for her friends. I remember it so clearly that it hurts; that's the difference between us. The way things have happened to me while parenting, the way they continue to happen, all my memories of it run together, feel like a life lived in slowed-down present tense.

The kids are getting to ages and levels of awareness where they can see how having the baby has rocked me, but they can't put a name to it, and they instinctively humor me by spending little bits of time with me, sitting beside me on the couch, gingerly, speaking softly to me like I'm an aging relative. I tell my second son the premise of this show, and he watches for a few minutes before wandering off. When I look at them, I see all the past thems, all their shadow selves, faces smeared with Fudgesicles, underwear so small it could fit on a doll. My daughter is born in an impossibly painful series of minutes, and then she is living with me through entire days, through the sun rising and falling, through cycles of the moon, through seasons. She was nothing, then she was, is, a whole person.

Is a day I spend in this haze a wasted day? I try to focus on all the times I breastfeed her and change her, the naps she takes in the carrier while I fold laundry and prep vegetables for dinner and walk around the neighborhood, first with a slight limp, then with a dull, deep pulling sensation, and then finally, feeling probably as normal as I'm ever going to feel, with a ghostlike pain, a whisper of what it was in the exact same place, the place where she left my imagination and entered the real world.

In the photographs accompanying a November 2020 profile, Ina Garten looks stunningly beautiful in her garden. In her trademark blue button-down and a red scarf, she stares directly at the camera, her lush brown hair falling in light curls, her hands gently cradling a small batch of on-the-vine cherry tomatoes. Some of the tomatoes are a dark pink brown, others a vibrant green. Garten is in her seventies, and in this photograph, she looks unbelievably robust.

She's how old? Anna asks. I tilt my phone at her and show her the photo. *Isn't she beautiful?* I ask. I look into Anna's face. It's been two full years since I sat on the couch watching Ina's early seasons with our fourth, our last, baby. Anna is in her forties now, and she's recently started wearing glasses full-time, something I began doing myself in the fourth grade. We don't own any serums or skin creams. Anna doesn't wear makeup, doesn't do anything to her face other than wash it, and she has deep wrinkles around her eyes, around her mouth. Time comes at us and we let it. Anna has a septum ring and harsh, short, salt-and-pepper bangs. She is a tough, very middle-aged-looking lady. Every year, she looks harder and gayer and more herself. She's wearing gray denim overalls and plastic earrings shaped like fishbowls. I love that when I look closely at my wife, I can see, in some ways, all that's passed between us. Whenever I joke about how I looked when she met me, all that awkward girlishness, the times I wore my hair down or wore skirts, she snaps back, *I didn't even have bangs yet, and you fell in love with me!* We are in a coffee shop, sitting at a counter, and I'm interrupting her over and over and reading her portions of Ina Garten's 2024 memoir, *Be Ready When the Luck Happens*. When I pause for a moment between passages, we look at the cover photo together. *I want to show you my favorite photo of Ina*, I say, and I open my phone to the garden photograph.

In the accompanying profile, Julia Moskin writes about her years of puzzling over Garten's fame as if following a compulsion: *As a reporter*, Moskin writes, *I have spent a lot of time over the same years wondering exactly how a wealthy white woman with no unique culinary skill or television shtick built such a diverse and devoted following.*

On April 1, 2020, Moskin writes, *she posted a video of herself making a Cosmopolitan cocktail that begins with a full liter of vodka and ends with her sipping out of a martini glass as tall as a garden gnome.*

By the time the cosmo video aired, Garten had been on television for nearly twenty years, though one could say its virality marked a resurgence for Garten and connected her to a new generation of aspirant home chefs.

In the coffee shop, five years after the video flew into my inbox again and again and again, I pull it up on my phone to show Anna. As Garten dumps endless ounces of liquor and juices into the giant pitcher, telling us, *You never know who's going to stop by . . . wait a minute, nobody's stopping by!* and then asking, *I mean, how easy is this?* we laugh together. When Garten first posted it, weeks after I'd been sent home from the clinic and began working at the dining room table, I was falling deep and hard down the food creator rabbit hole, but I didn't share that with Anna. Part of the privacy of this obsession is that Anna doesn't really give a shit about any of it—the food or the people whose lives revolve around it. She has maybe one drink a month, can't remember what she ate for breakfast, let alone the last one thousand weeknight dinners, and she doesn't covet a beautiful kitchen in the Hamptons or even a pristine set of sturdy white plates for entertaining. She's never watched Stella Parks or Sara Moulton. She thinks Alison Roman is cute but that doesn't put dinner on our table. Ina Garten transcends all that. We laugh together about a video of a seventy-year-old woman making a gallon-size cocktail all for herself.

My parents bought their place in the Hamptons when I was in college. It is, if not the most beautiful house I've ever seen, certainly the most gorgeous place I've ever been inside. Each of the handful of times we've gone *to Long Island*, as we instinctively, euphemistically refer to these trips, Anna and I enter an alternate universe. In this universe, I must perform the same tasks as always—changing diapers, flipping pancakes—but in a breathtaking setting. While nudging a stain off one of the glasses my siblings and I will use for another round of post-bedtime palomas, I can stand at the counter looking directly out my parents' patio door at the Peconic Bay. The kitchen has the kinds of appliances Ina Garten has in her own Hamptons home. They're top of the line and blend in with the cabinets. In the Hamptons grocery store, I buy Cinnamon Toast Crunch, Oscar Mayer bacon, Arnold bread—all the same things I would at home, only everything is marked up a bit, and everyone in the store is wearing flip-flops and looks tanned and beaten by the sun and by nights of drinking too much.

Soon after my parents began spending time on Long Island, my mother called. She didn't want to talk to me, she wanted to talk to my second son, who was in preschool. *You'll never believe who I saw!* she yelled into the other end. *The Barefoot Contessa! She was on a boat!*

I don't think it's the ease of her recipes, some of which are in my slightly-fancy-dinner rotation—her Baked Cod with Garlic & Herb Ritz Croutons, her Portobello Mushroom Lasagna, her Challah French Toast, which is flush with orange zest—that keeps me watching. Julia Moskin supposes that people are mainly attracted to Garten because she is willing to admit that cooking isn't easy, that she still struggles. This endears viewers to her, making us want to follow along with her extremely specific measurements, knowing we'll never have to follow instinct or season "to taste."

But for me, this isn't it. It isn't the recipes. It's her life. It's the money, the house, the kitchen where staples never run out and where cheese from a specialty shop isn't a once-a-year splurge. There's a part of me that wants a garden, though I don't want to have to care for it myself. I bet Ina Garten and her husband, Jeffrey, don't spend endless hours lying next to each other in bed sending Zillow links to modest-yet-still-unreachable real estate in every corner of the United States. *We could never afford this*, one of us might say, hitting *send* on a property where our biggest win might be gaining the ability to shower in a restroom where a child hasn't just taken a shit. Or maybe we'd actually have a closet for each kid. And I know what I just said, that my parents have a house in the place where Garten lives, and I said a house because it's not their only house, but this wealth, which raised me and lives adjacent to me, there's still a distance from it, I think, every time I try to buy used sneakers or a child's bicycle off a neighbor, for as cheap as I can.

I don't want to own a specialty foods store on Long Island, or to have my own long-running television show, or to write thirteen best-selling cookbooks. So, what do I want? Some measure of peace, I imagine. Garten didn't come up with the name Barefoot Contessa, the moniker she's used on television and in her thirteen cookbooks. At thirty, she was not into the direction her life was headed in and found a solution in real estate. She purchased a specialty foods store in Westhampton named after the owner, an Italian woman who'd been called Barefoot Contessa in childhood, after the Bogart film. Garten hadn't gone to culinary school, had no experience in the food business, though she'd had a number of jobs—in a women's clothing store, at a bookstore, in the back office of a strip club—before taking the job she hated the most, the one that made her want to escape her life so badly that a store in a place she'd never visited cried out to her from the back of the paper.

That last job was at the White House Office of Management and Budget, where she worked in the legislative office, specializing in nuclear policy. Though the job was *pretty heady stuff*, the day-to-day quickly became an arduous bore. Garten writes in her memoir, *The big-picture issues were interesting, and there was a great sense of urgency when we stayed all night at the office to get every detail right before sending legislation, or a budget, off to the White House. But after that, the slow-moving process was an obstacle course lined with glue, and I found that deeply frustrating.*

In this time of deep, existential boredom—*Am I dead yet?* Garten remembers asking herself at her desk in Washington—I see the Garten I most relate to, most deeply desire to understand. She turns to decorating her home and, even more than that, to cooking and entertaining, to give her the stimulation so lacking in her career.

In my favorite passages of the memoir, Garten learns the ins and outs of running Barefoot Contessa, which, under her leadership, becomes a Hamptons destination. There's a delightful chaos in her descriptions of her early days at the store. *Every day at Barefoot Contessa was different*, she writes. A customer buys ten pounds of grilled lemon chicken for her cat. An employee needs a ride to the emergency room when she slices her hand cutting a bagel. Garten drives around New York City at three in the morning on Wednesdays to buy from her favorite suppliers.

We think of Ina Garten as someone whose marriage has completely defined her life, but she writes that when she started her new chapter as a business owner, she considered divorcing Jeffrey. In the seventies, she didn't have models for how she could balance the chaotic ambition needed to succeed owning a seasonal bust-and-boom food store. Because Jeffrey had been the only constant in her world, he helped her move into the little apartment she rented on her own during their brief separation. After therapy and negotiations over their roles in the marriage and in each other's lives, they reconciled and moved back in together. *When I bought Barefoot Contessa*, she writes, *I shattered our traditional roles—took a baseball bat to them and left them in pieces.*

Watching Garten makes me think, inevitably, about the decisions I might have made had I not made the foundational decision of my own early twenties: to have children. Anna has her vision of a life without them, and I can see her vision clearly. But for me, parenting was what gave me futurity. I only began to envision myself growing old in its context.

Anna and I are both neurodivergent, and we're coming to know what it means to figure that out in middle age, at the particularly stressful intersection of parenting and contemporary American life. And we identify with this feeling Garten had when she took over the store, that the only thing that could possibly help ground you is blowing up your whole life, starting over somewhere else. Anna and I struggled less when we were young, when we could worry only about ourselves, and when everything important happened on paper. If only I was born decades earlier, I think, and each child did not have a separate app, let alone multiple apps, which would notify me of their missing homework, of their diaper changes, of their track practices. I don't think in these moments of overwhelm about the fact that if I'd been born a generation earlier, I might not be living an open trans life, might not have my family at all. Who has time for rational thinking about queerness and progress when you're tired and lost in the thick of the endless to-do forest? I just think I want to be less tired at bedtime. If we were still doing strips of paper in a school folder, maybe I wouldn't feel like every day was just a new vat of quicksand for both of us to sink into.

Garten has given us so many cakes, so many roast chickens, so much abundance, she has a job where you can constantly reinvent yourself and make new things. I'm looking for myself in Ina Garten and I see a woman who is bored and overwhelmed in equal measure by the endless onslaught of tasks involved in many versions of contemporary life. *Am I dead yet?* I became a teacher to talk fast and work on my feet. I'm reading Garten's memoir in a coffee shop on Anna's birthday, and one of Ina Garten's cakes awaits us at home. I made the cake last night, birthday eve. Beatty's Chocolate Cake has a few things that make it stand out from other cakes I make. For one, there aren't metric units, so I can't use a scale. You just have to scoop and hope, but it works every time. Both the cake and its topping call for more coffee than most other chocolate baked goods, and yet it's not too much—a cup of hot coffee in the batter, a full tablespoon of instant coffee in the frosting.

It's been five years since the early pandemic, and last night, when I opened the instant coffee can that's been sitting on my shelf for who knows how long, I was flooded with the smell of the whipped coffees we made each afternoon during lockdown, to hurry the day along. Before this baby, before the reality of her, before even wanting her.

A woman I do not know leaves a copy of *The Barefoot Contessa Cookbook*, Ina Garten's 1999 debut, on her front stoop. I have won it in a random selection on my local Buy Nothing Facebook group, where I enter lotteries for fleece jackets, toy organizers, children's Crocs, and then this book, one of the few Garten titles my mother hasn't purchased for me, hasn't sent me through the mail for a birthday or a Christmas.

Before the plague years, you'd stand on the stoop, or even on the sidewalk, chatting for a bit during these exchanges. *So does this mean you bought a new bicycle? How old was your kid when he used this scooter? Does he go to the school over there on the corner?* But now, it's customary to arrange a pickup time and to leave the item to be claimed, with the mutual understanding that no friendship will arise from the interaction. On the cover of the cookbook, the hint of a blue oxford in the background, a small slice of a right hand, two serving spoons tossing her Provençal Potato Salad, a *wonderful summer afternoon lunch*. In the book, Melanie Acevedo's hypersaturated photographs emphasize the colorful bounty of the Hamptons, that place we both know, where Ina Garten was not born but which she would come to love and, to some of us, represent.

This photography embodies the style that would carry Garten through her career. While my constant reinventions often come with new looks, new hair, new jacket, mustache, no mustache, another tattoo, another piercing, Ina Garten has only locked down on the way she looks.

On my most deluded days, what I think would help me most isn't therapy or medication or a time machine or a different life but a uniform. Ina Garten has one. She wears solid, crisp button-down shirts, sometimes black, occasionally white, nearly always a shade of blue. At a few months postpartum, I don't like the way I look. It's not that I don't look how I did in some magical before, let's be real, I don't have that, a past of looking a way I wanted. It's just that I don't know how to dress this particular body, the post-transition, postpartum body. I wear beaten-to-hell Old Navy elastic-waist pants, size large, that I wore constantly when I was pregnant. Now I'm not, but I don't know what to buy next. What body will I have in a month, in a year? I want Ina Garten to tell me when she felt like the body she had was, if not permanent, at least settled enough. I wear button-downs, open and arranged in a way that I hope obscures my lactating chest. I wear loose sports bras, and every once in a while, I let myself bind for an hour. On the days when the shirt I wear over all that mess is blue, like Ina's, I admit I do feel better.

In the introduction to that first cookbook, published before her celebrity really took off, Garten writes, *Food at Barefoot Contessa, I soon found out, is about more than dinner. It's about coming home and being taken care of. It's about Mom. I actually think that the food our mothers made may not be what we are nostalgic for. It's more an emotional picture of a mother who was always there, knew what we needed, loved us, let us run free when we wanted to explore. Food is about nurturing: not only physical but also emotional nurturing.*

Ina Garten famously does not have children. In the introductory monologue of the Ina Garten episode of her podcast *Wiser Than Me*, a show in which she interviews older women, Julia Louis-Dreyfus begins by talking about her childhood love of desserts, which leads her into talking about baking for her own children as an act of maternal giving: *When our kids were little, providing for them, obviously, this is some instinctual maternal thing, you just get this incredible joy out of your kids finishing a meal that you made for them, right, the most basic kind of nurturing.*

Louis-Dreyfus goes on to describe the birthday cake she has made year after year for her son, something that fits with her sense that she is *captive to ritual.*

In my favorite moment of the interview, Garten says that Jeffrey encouraged her to do something with her life that would be fun. *He said it for me particularly because if it's fun, I want to do it. If it's not fun, you can't get me to do it with the cattle prod.*

Half a century after high school graduation, Garten remembers a high school physics teacher who wrote on the bottom of every assignment, *Have fun at all costs.*

So many of Garten's food rituals surround her husband, Jeffrey. In episode after episode, she serves him food that reminds her of something they did together: when she mailed him brownies at college, when they traveled in Paris together. She cooks for his returns from business trips and for holidays, birthdays, the Fourth of July, and, most important of all, Thanksgiving.

And she cooks for her friends. In season 9's "Halloween for Grownups," Garten serves pork loin, homemade applesauce, and espresso martinis, made in a batch recipe that calls for, all told, three cups of liquor and two cups of espresso. So it interests me that Louis-Dreyfus begins by talking about making her child an orange cream cheese cake to introduce Ina Garten, someone who, above perhaps anything else, has become a symbol of how full life without children can be.

Was it hard to decide whether to have children?

It wasn't a struggle at all, Garten tells Louis-Dreyfus. *I had no interest in having children. None. I just had a terrible childhood. And it was nothing I wanted to re-create.*

On a 2021 episode of Al Roker's *Cooking Up a Storm*, Garten pinpoints more specifically how her childhood led her into cooking. *I think what I was craving as a child*, she says, *was connecting with people, and I felt that if you feed them, they always show up and you have a good time together. That was the connection I loved, so I kept doing it over and over again.*

In her memoir, Garten describes her childhood as a cold and lonely life. As an adult, she's discussed this with her brother: *Ken and I agree that our parents were not people who should have had children.*

School, for Garten, was an *alternate universe*, where she was busy and popular. She found herself in a vibrant social group. *They were all smart and fun and I felt alive when we were together.*

In an interview with David Remnick, Garten says, of her mother: *My mother was very—I think now I might say that she would be diagnosed with Asperger's. Didn't have relationships, and she had no interest in food, so she would get dinner on the table, but there was no joy in it.*

D*idn't have relationships* is the phrase chiming again and again as I flip through my stack of ten cookbooks by Garten. Born in 1948, she uses language around disability that I can't expect to be perfect. But it stings, seeing this connection laid bare: that to be neurodivergent is to have no relationships, to fail to connect.

Anna and I make people like us. They look like us, but that's only where the likeness begins. Our children are developmentally delayed, do not conform to the checklists and schedules devised by child development specialists who work for universities and government agencies and state entities and school districts. I knew these checklists, these generic goals for generic children, long before I had my own. After reading about their racist histories in college, their flaws and limitations, I made my living off them as a special education teacher. I didn't believe in these evaluations, not fully, but I was just a little person working in big swirling systems, an agent for this machinery, and I lived by the checklists. In schools around Philadelphia, I sat across from other people's children and showed them flip cards of words and math facts, of a kind that were shown to so many in my family of origin, and then to my own children, and finally, to me.

Kids are not boring, but that part of the work was, calculating the degree to which a child adhered to expectations of growth and development. I'd use the half days, when the school's schedule was wonky to begin with, to pull the children out of a busy classroom and into an empty one where I sat with the flip cards and scrap paper and scoring sheets. These half days felt longer than any regular day, in which I taught children reading and math in small groups, sometimes inside their regular classroom, sometimes in the library or in the classroom I shared with another teacher. What if I could have spent that half day with a child doing a fun project?

In the 1970s, when she worked at the Nuclear Regulatory Commission, Ina Garten felt a similar malaise. At night, she threw dinner parties. I, too, have cooked through it all: evaluations, determination meetings, doctors' appointments, therapy sessions, intervention meetings. The stacks of paper, evidence of all that is wrong with us, all the things we cannot do. How would it have changed Ina Garten's life to have a name for her mother's difference from her, from her friends, from other people in their lives? Can a label recast the difficult parts of your past?

On one occasion after another, Anna and I sit side by side in our home or in a prekindergarten classroom or, most often, in a conference room located beside the main office in various elementary schools to review documents. The script is flipped, and I am not the professional. In these meetings, I play the role of the parent. I listen instead of explain. In these rooms, we hear white women talk. They discuss observation data, test results, the extent of our children's delays, often, especially in the early years, expressed as percentages deviated from a norm. We read the words: *mild*, *moderate*, *severe*, *profound*. On evaluation days, we present our children to a team to be put through the tests. When they are very young, it's cute, in a way, seeing them asked to walk or jump or play with blocks. I think about what they're wearing to school on those days, about how clean our house is, about what it means to be a normal family. I remember how many people think trans men should not have children. My own family, my family of origin, looked normal in most ways, but then there were those of us who deviated enough to need these tests too. The white women ask me and Anna to talk about our children, what they can and cannot do. Have we seen them obey traffic laws? Put on a pair of pants on their own? And did those pants have zippers or snaps? I describe the way one of my children lays the soles of the shoes atop the feet, knowing that sticking a foot inside the shoe is still out of reach. As my answers come out of my mouth, I question in real time whether I am exaggerating what I perceive as the ways they diverge from other children, from normal children. By the time we have the fourth baby, we have so thoroughly absorbed these checklists and charts that we have to consciously remind ourselves to look past them to see the child, her perfect rubbery wrists, her open-mouthed smile, that happy toothy O.

It's not just that we sit there. It's that we participate actively in othering our children, just as I prompted parents to do when I ran evaluation meetings. You had to ask in a way that didn't imply you were qualified to diagnose anything, or even suggest it. *Is there any relevant documentation from your child's physician that would assist our team? Has any healthcare provider expressed concern about your child's development?* For us, it began in the pediatrician's office: we showed her a video of our first child, who had never sat steadily, who was not yet standing up when his brother was born, tripping over objects that were not there inside a coffee shop. Step, step, thud. Step, step, thud.

With every child Anna and I have, there is a new stack of paper that comes home. We place the papers into folders, the folders into a big plastic bin next to its sibling folders.

School teams combine our responses to their questions with their own, forming a sort of family narrative:

described by [ ] mother on the day of the evaluation as a pleasant and happy child

conveys frustration by screaming, pulling or shoving toys, and at times biting

is judged to present with some tactile avoidant behaviors at this time

at times saliva can be observed on [ ] lower lip

strengths and interests include math, gaming, playing the piano and cello, and reading science-fiction and fantasy stories

is often polite and cooperative in class

displays marked impairment

prefers to wear sweatpants and t-shirts

sits at the front and center of the classroom, at a table with three other students

likes solo leisure activities

is sincere, diligent

understands that multiplication is repeated addition

is a motivated communicator

is a curious student and catches on to new material quickly

errors were noted on the following sounds: l, sh, ch, b, t, d, g, th, r, j, v, y, z, vocalic r (or, er, air), and s-, l-l, and r-blends

becomes preoccupied with thoughts, forgetting what else is going on

was tongue-tied as an infant and struggled with breast feeding

Mr. and Mrs. Belc share that as a baby [ ] was attached to them and affectionate with them

Mr. Belc's ratings fell within the Markedly Atypical range, indicating a very significant problem

father shared that he thinks this is getting in the way of [ ] ability to get to know new people

the family feels that [ ] becomes frustrated when [ ] is not understood

parent endorsements on the Practical domain fell in the Low range overall

Mr. Belc reported that [ ] often intends to do [ ] chores, but does not have a good sense of how long things take

Dad attended the meeting by phone. He expressed concerns with the progress in speech

parent input, provided by email:

struggles to "get going"

needs additional prompts

will sometimes sit "doing nothing"

struggled . . . with using technology appropriately

In the nearly five years I first took testosterone, before I went off to get pregnant again, I almost never cried. I watched so many transition videos in the years before I began taking T, and what I loved most of all was the voices, their slow creep away from the original. They maintained a shadow of what they'd been, but only that. I listened to the men talk, loved the way their voices cracked, loved the way they all used the same inflection to say, *This is my voice one month on T. This is my voice six months on T.* I fell in love with the trans voice, and then, all of a sudden, I got to have one. The men did not talk about the feeling you get when sadness builds inside but has no way out. Some nights while Anna worked, I sat on a laptop trying to find something that would prompt a release: Oscar speeches, Obama speeches, tear-jerker movies, videos of people winning championships or falling at the finish line or sustaining career-ending injuries. I gained so much taking the medication but worried I lost something too. Despair, release. I was handsomer, stronger, but there was a level of feeling I could no longer touch. It's weird to say I regret losing my ability to cry. Each week, I did this to myself, injecting the thick oil into my stomach, halting that swell of feeling. And then, I stopped the shots, to have the last baby.

I go back on testosterone when the baby is five months old. All those nights lying awake, crying, wondering what would help me, and on one of those nights, Anna finally took me by both shoulders and said, *I know what will help you. Take. Testosterone.*

After two months back on my injections, I don't cry as much, but I still do sometimes. For example, I tear up watching my older daughter sing in her choir concert at our local school. I am there alone, to watch my daughter in her choir and my second son in his. Across town, Anna and the baby watch our oldest play the cello in his middle school concert. In the school three blocks south from our house, I sit in a beat-up auditorium stuffed with plastic chairs a local organization rented for the occasion. I am at the end of a long row full of one family: two adults and three teenage boys. The boys hold little bouquets of flowers for the girl they have come to see. She is in the first grade, like my daughter. The room is so crowded it feels like everyone in the neighborhood must be here. All that chattering and catching up, a nervous excitement that's in every room where people gather, since the months when nobody did. And then it is, for a moment, silent before the singing begins. A week ago, I put my smart phone in a drawer and closed the drawer, and so all I can do is wait and look down at my hands, and then up again at my daughter. She wears a cornflower sweater and her hair is in braids. She looks, suddenly, like my mother-in-law, who died when she was a toddler. My daughter's skin is darker than our other children's, tan even in the winter. Her slate eyes, the thin sandy hair, the wide, toothy smile. My daughter sings confidently, smiling the whole time. She stares directly into the middle of the audience because she has not seen where I am sitting, off to the side. I like seeing her when she cannot see me. Her mouth opens wide and words pour out. I can see her teeth from all the way over here. My daughter is seven years old.

Just before this daughter's second birthday, I am stirring bolognese in my parents' kitchen. We're staying with them in suburban New Jersey for a while, to be closer to Anna's mother, who is sick with a fatal brain tumor. She's at work at her travel nursing job in Manhattan, and I am listening to the War on Drugs and cooking one of our favorite meals. I've never met someone who isn't a vegetarian who doesn't love this pasta sauce. This kitchen, my mother's kitchen, is gorgeous: six huge gas burners, two ovens, countertops wherever you turn. I know that my daughter is in the room. I feel her behind me. She is an easy toddler usually, so quiet and compliant. I don't know where the other two are, but it's okay, because they are old enough to wander, to entertain themselves. Unless I hear screaming, I don't need to worry about them. My daughter is so calm that I bring her to my office hours and put her on the floor with a single toy and she will sit while I work grading papers, making PowerPoint presentations, reading journal articles. She will eat a granola bar and touch my office mates' books with her small, pudgy hands. She will spin a swivel chair. My daughter is my main companion because her brothers attend school or otherwise occupy each other. She and I go to the library and quietly read books on the floor. She flips through them slowly, touching each picture. I bring her to the coffee shop we both love and buy her a cookie and tell her *I love you* and I say her whole name before I take a bite and she smiles and says nothing. She cannot talk at all, and she is a mostly silent child.

No recipe I know makes the house smell better. I am thinking about how quickly the sauce will reduce, how much water I may need to add, when, standing at the stove, I hear crinkling and I turn around and my daughter is holding a plastic bag of pills. All the cabinets are closed and my heart is wild, tearing apart my parents' kitchen looking for where they came from. My little sister's backpack is slumped over and unzipped in a corner. *What did you do?* I ask our baby. The bag is open. *What did you take?* But I know she won't say anything. Of course she says nothing. My parents' house is huge and there are so many people living here right now, and nothing is childproofed. I use my hands to open my daughter's mouth, sticking my probably dirty fingers under her little tongue. I smear onion and garlic juice, tomatoes I broke apart by hand, sweeping in a circular motion, looking for the pills. You're not supposed to do that, not supposed to dig around in their mouths, lest you push something farther down the kid's throat. But I am panicking. My daughter gags. She cries when I scream at my sister on the phone. My sister is still a kid too. *What do you mean you don't know how many pills were in the bag?* I want my sister to say this is her fault because then it can't be my fault, can't be because I was not paying enough attention to my children. There are times I'm just so in it when I'm cooking, you know? It is the one thing that can hold my attention more than anything else. That narrowed focus on chopping carrots just so, on watching for meat to reach the exact correct shade of brown. Some of the pills, my sister says, are Motrin and some are not, some are anxiety meds and some are depression meds, and though I have been depressed and anxious most of my life, I have never taken any of these medications, in my family only the people who need them most do, even though we all struggle, and so I do not know what any of the medications my sister names do or look like, and within minutes of hanging up on my her, not before I can scream at her a little more for good measure, my daughter and I are in the car racing to the local ER and I hate to admit this, but I am thinking first of all about what I will say to the person doing registration and intake. I know what testosterone has done to my voice. Now I sound gay and soft and unsure of myself. Anna would know what to do, she's cis and has a hard-to-place accent other people find alluring, and she can talk herself into or out of any situation in the world. I want to stay home in the kitchen, and instead, I take my poisoned daughter up to the counter. I am wishing I could stir the sauce and think about whatever I think about for the three hours it takes to make bolognese.

Around this time, our daughter's pediatrician tells us what we already know: it is time to call Early Intervention because she has not begun to speak. By age two, most children have over fifty words. A child who does not is deemed a *late talker*. According to Michelle MacRoy-Higgins and Carlyn Kolker, *Late talkers are usually identified when they produce fewer than 50 words and do not combine words into short sentences around their second birthday. Research has shown that late talkers do not ever catch up completely.* How important is it to catch up, how would we know the answer to that? Anna and I go back and forth about whether the sound she makes when thirsty—*guh*—counts as a word. Do any of the sounds in *guh* exist in water? We say *water* again and again, finding new texture in it each time. Anna is from Warsaw and then New York and then Philadelphia and then she is from where we are when our daughter should be but is not speaking, Michigan's Upper Peninsula. And I am from New York and then New Jersey and then Philadelphia and then Michigan too. We say *wooder* like Philadelphians, we think the *oo* in *wood* is like the *uh* in *guh*. We reach this conclusion before meeting the county's early childhood speech and language pathologist, who is to come to our home to evaluate our daughter. In the hour before she arrives, we placate the children with television and clean everything in the house to seem more normal. *Mandated reporter cleaning*, we've come to call this, as more of our children needed home visits from evaluators and therapists. In the moments I am supposed to be most focused on my children, in their moments of deepest vulnerability and judgment, my attention wavers and I center myself. Will the speech and language pathologist know that I—that our family—is queer? I most often look in the mirror just before meeting a new person, to see how likely it is that they will clock me. Always the same question and no answer, just me searching others' faces to see, somehow, if they are searching mine. If they know, then they will probably think my kids need whatever kind of therapy because I am their parent. Anna and I decide *guh* is a word, that our daughter has a single, precious word. But when we report our findings to the speech pathologist, she just frowns.

The sublingual space is beneath the tongue, an area containing salivary glands but also empty space, open air beneath muscle. While reading anatomy texts, I see it referred to as *potential space*. When I sit with my daughter during her speech therapy, I watch her mouth move and think about the potential Anna and I are banking on. Her future of speaking, singing even. What gave us the right to decide on goals for someone else? To realize her potential, the thinking goes, she must learn to speak. Then I think about all the things I could be doing while the therapist models how she moves her tongue to make each sound. I could be writing, doing dishes, doing laundry, making dinner. The therapist and my daughter color a unicorn. The therapist asks if the color my daughter selects is really called *gleen*. She leans into the camera and opens her mouth. I am sitting on my work computer while my daughter says the same words over and over, words with *sh* in the middle: *marshmallow*, *mushroom*, *milkshake*. Each is to be put in a sentence. *So many foods today*, my daughter says. Her voice is weary. I try not to count or even think about the hours of her little life that pass this way, drilling these sounds over and over again.

When childless friends ask us if they should have children, Anna almost always says yes, and I almost always say no. *Do you like your life?* I ask. It's not a rhetorical question. I really do want to hear the answer. If you really love your life, maybe you won't love having children. I didn't like my life when I was twenty-four and Anna was pregnant with our first kid. I was working in the basement of a Philadelphia high school. That year, I taught eleven intellectually disabled teens and young adults. Like parenting, teaching often feels like a series of the longest, hardest days imaginable strung together to make a beautiful something. Though periodically I felt soaring accomplishment or warmth, it's often only years later that I can realize what happened, how the experience changed me. I hated that my students had to learn in a basement classroom overrun by mice and that their buses dropped them off at a different entrance than their abled peers. I hated how much of their time they spent stuck with me and loved when they got to go out and work with other teachers too. What I remember most are not the things I learned about how to craft lessons and activities that would include my students, whose ages and interests and abilities spanned a vast gap, though I learned and tried a lot. We took the city bus together. We went to the grocery store and to Walmart. In the classroom, my students and I read the news and watched the days and weeks and months of the year go by. We got new haircuts and jewelry and talked about our homes and families. We sat in small groups reading and doing math.

If I wrote out all the years of my life on a timeline and you asked me if that one was good, what would I say? The truth is that I tried to leave those students, applied for a job in another school in October. I would teach teens with "lower-impact" disabilities—learning disabilities, executive functioning deficits, etc.—study skills, helping them with their projects and papers for other classes. It was work that I already knew how to do and would do well. I applied in a moment of weakness and I felt horrible about the day I took off from work for the interview. I sat on the subway fretting, continued to do so even as I emerged in a different neighborhood, a nicer one than where I worked, and walked to the building. What were my students doing all day with the sub, without me there? Looking back so many years later, I realize that maybe they didn't care that I wasn't there. I wasn't that important, and I wasn't even that good of a teacher.

I tried to leave my students, but in the end I stayed. I was twenty-four years old and lost in the world. I thought I should try to find meaning outside of work, thinking that would help. There were weekends I spent in the kitchen, just like Ina Garten, making Julia Child dishes—her coq au vin, her boeuf bourguignon. Any extra money I had, I spent on herbs and expensive cuts of meat. I was trying to find a way to have fun at any cost, like Garten's teacher told her to do. These were meals that trashed our tiny galley kitchen, that used every pot and pan, every knife and spoon. It was an epic mess, but if you make an epic mess, then that's the only mess in front of you.

One Friday, I stood in line at the local grocery shop thinking about the time I would spend, with our sharpest paring knife, peeling pearl onions. I began to see how I was using food to speed up time. There was an anger I was turning away from, anger that I wasn't a better adult, anger that you can't speed that up, you can't grow up on the timeline you choose. Before Anna got pregnant with our first baby, in the months when we were trying to make it happen, there was a night I got drunk and we fought in a bar near our apartment, and then as she walked away from me on the street, I started yelling at her, acting in a way that anyone could plainly see was angry and aggressive, before I realized: I teach in this city, I can't act like this in public. Was it because I didn't want a student or their parent to see me, or because I knew I had work I needed to do on myself? And then a baby was coming. That year was so complicated. Anna was in nursing school and she was pregnant. She wasn't ever sick or tired or in pain. She was happy. Our social circle was relatively small, especially since our decision to have kids years before our peers scared some of them away. And so, aside from the time I spent with her and my gym friends, I spent almost all my time with disabled people. My eleven students, rowdy and funny and tiring.

And that was the thing I noticed most that year, how my perception of how to relate to people changed the less time I spent with abled adults. So I wasn't growing up on the timeline I expected, so what? I was on my own timeline. With my students, I made sandwiches, parfaits, cupcakes, and fruit salads. Cooking was part of the work of the classroom, and so I got reimbursed for groceries. I was teaching them to follow multistep directions. To use household tools. To read a simple recipe. To perform expected social behaviors at classroom gatherings. My sense of what people were like was shaped by these students, whose lives were defined and confined by their diagnoses and the percentiles into which they'd fallen. To me, they were just them, just people, not because of any mighty anti-ableism deep inside me, not because I'm inherently good, but just because this was who I spent all my time with. We were trapped together, and we were not that different, since that was the basic thing that defined most of our waking hours. The metrics that failed to hold them failed to hold me too—I began to see that. But I still wasn't happy most of the time. You can't see the transformation as it's happening, especially when you're waiting for it. I was immature and unfocused, and I wished I was better at my job, but I wasn't ready to put in the work, not the hours but the deep work it takes to be really, truly good at teaching. The decision to have children came for me because I couldn't sit still in the way I needed to, and I searched for something else to throw my life into.

People don't tend to talk about whether having kids is fun or not, or how the fun of your life, supposing it still exists, is different from the way it was before.

I have read Sarah Manguso's essay on becoming a mother, "The Grand Shattering," on a number of occasions, and each time I react differently to its arguments. Manguso describes a trepidation through her twenties and thirties, a horror even, at the idea of having children, of what it would do to her need to write, her need for space to think. She then writes of a transformation when she has her child, a shifting in what she sees as the point of her life. Before motherhood, she believed her work, writing books, which took up a tremendous amount of time and energy, could save lives. *But the point of motherhood*, Manguso writes, *is to help someone immediately, to console a person who is right there next to you.*

The point of having a child is to be rent asunder, torn in two.

In an interview two years later, Manguso says, *I wouldn't say that I made the good decision or the right decision. Those words don't feel like what I'm trying to articulate—they seem sort of off to the side of it. In writing "The Grand Shattering," I was certain that something had happened. And what had happened was that I changed my mind.*

She is in conversation with Sheila Heti and Rachel Zucker on the latter's podcast. Zucker is a mother, and Heti is not. When Manguso says, *I can't deny that I, I take up less space in space, and I take up less time in the time, and that much of what I do in a day can easily be filed under the words "sacrifice" and "service,"* she quickly begins arguing with herself: *Actually*, she says, *I'm not smaller than I was, perhaps I'm larger.*

She stops again. *But small and large, again, just seem like they're not really descriptive of what has actually happened.*

The people I consider my closest friends don't have four children. They have no children or they have one or two. There are aspects of my life, of my decision-making and relentless follow-through, that these friends will never understand. I have to believe things are going to turn around after my own unexpected grand shattering. I wanted to be pregnant again, to give birth again. I wanted my older kids to have a younger sibling, and they wanted it too. I wanted a loud dinner table and a lot of opinions. I wanted chaos. I wanted, and thought I would get, a fun time, a fun life.

Maybe the fact that I was already a parent when I transitioned serves as a barrier to imagining a life in which I did not have children, or did not have this number of children. To move back and continue on the path I was on—it's not conceivable. Would it have been enough just to want to be myself, or did I need to have the motivator of children watching me, of needing to model the life I wanted to live for them?

But I see Anna, in a life in which I do not cook for her. Anna is still tall and beautiful but maybe she is not aging so fast without me and our kids. Everything could be different. She could spend more money on her hair or clothes instead of on us. She could have jewelry and a small car that's not full of our junk. She'd play Roller Derby and maybe kiss a lot of women. Maybe she has a husband and maybe a wife and maybe not, maybe kids and maybe not. It took her years after we had the first one to understand that she had been far from ready to be a mother, to give her life over to other people that way. It was in the early-adult years that she stepped out into the world in the wrong way. She wishes she had lived with roommates first. Where she lived, in West Philadelphia, most people we knew lived with a group of housemates, who shared a kitchen and a chore wheel and jam jars they used for water and wine. Anna wishes she'd gotten a dog in her twenties, like all the other women we know. She'd take him to the park and talk to other queers about all his needs, the way he liked to be pet or handled. Instead, she let me barrel ahead. It was me who was driven to anchor myself to a full home.

Each summer when it is our first son's birthday, I make a strawberry cake and try not to remember all the days and nights Anna spent crying on our old brown couch because it was so hard after he was born. One day, I know, their birthdays will bring pure joy, not memories of cycles of depression and arduous adjustment to new life. Our son loves strawberries, always has. There is no diagnosis or growth chart that holds a candle to that reality, that he loves something I can give him. It doesn't matter that he started eating late, that he took slowly to it, that in the speech and language classroom he attended as a preschooler the teacher gave him the passive-aggressive Most Improved Award for finishing his lunch on time. When it's Anna's turn for dessert, to celebrate her birthday or a new job, or to make up for a bad day, or me just bucking up to say I am sorry I acted like an asshole, I make chocolate: brownies, quick cakes, pudding, cocoa sorbet, banana bread with chocolate chunks. I've come to crave those things too. In this way, our tastes are fused, have grown up together. Where do I begin and where does she end? We have never had separate adulthoods. I think about how she would decorate a bedroom, a kitchen. What would be in the refrigerator?

That is where my mind goes, even in this mental exercise of imagining a more expansive, more open life: inside the crisper drawers of a stainless steel refrigerator, inside an even narrower space within the space of the home.

On the cover of *Cooking for Jeffrey*, he holds a slice of layered chocolate cake and she holds him. On the inside, there is a picture of their Hamptons home, and on the next page, a picture of the Gartens on their wedding day. Ina is twenty. When I look at pictures of me when we took our first son home, after I had just turned twenty-five, I can barely handle how young I look, how unready for anything real.

In response to Manguso's musing about whether she has shrunken or grown, whether those are the correct ways of seeing her life, Heti says, *I covet the knowledge that you guys have, you know, and at the same time, I don't want to do any of those things that you guys have to do as mothers.* She's laughing as she says this.

What's the point in visiting and revisiting these conversations that women, who are usually white and usually wealthy and usually far older than I was when I already had multiple children of my own, have about whether or not they have children? I don't think I'm looking for meaning in someone else's life. I think I'm trying to see how my life relates, or doesn't, to theirs. Part of it is about the way they are able to express either their ease or difficulty in decision-making, the way pros and cons are presented, the way they can articulate their reasons. I have struggled to do just that. To be a trans man, to have children, these are not things that are supposed to happen to the same body, so I feel outside of the decision-making matrix in which these conversations occur.

In 1978, working in nuclear policy, Ina Garten realized, *There's got to be more to life than this!*, and she made a change. I, too, made a change, when I found that years in high school classrooms was not satisfying my life in any way. But I didn't buy a store, I didn't find a purpose; rather, I shrank from purpose, closed my world, began an insular family life. I had a child and then another and another. My world became the work of diapers and bottles and naptimes but also of therapies and norm charts. It was both what I would have expected and, as things always are when you introduce children into your life, totally unexpected.

Ina Garten remembers the first days of running a specialty foods store. They were hectic, and she didn't know what she was doing, but she loved it, at least, she loves it with the distance memory brings. And she remembers the end, eighteen years later, which kicked off the hardest year of her life. *One day*, she writes, *I was running a store with fifty employees and sometimes baking a thousand baguettes, and the next day, I literally had nothing to do*. This is when the second phrase of her career, the cookbooks and television shows, begins. I like that she is not a natural performer, not a natural cook. On every episode, she is the same—she is in her home, wearing her uniform—but she is also different, showing us yet another salad spin-off and cute table-scape. Garten tells David Remnick that she fired her television consultant after a single session. *Nothing she said made sense to me. I thought, I just need to be myself on TV. It's the only thing that works.*

I love that beautiful garden photograph of Garten from Julia Moskin's *New York Times* profile, taken by Christopher Simpson, and in fact I love most photographs I have seen of Garten, who is a powerful presence, onscreen and on the page, whose power has a magnetic hold on me, makes the world feel realer. It's the texture of the food and of her face. I can't decide whether I should read her memoir on paper or listen to it, so I do a little bit of both. It's not like me, but I find myself ignoring any criticism of the way she talks about the freedom she felt to make choices, freedom that, you know, you can only really enjoy if you have enough cash on hand to buy a whole store. Like so many, I find myself focusing on her love for Jeffrey, and how frank she is about navigating early-adult life with him, and trying to figure out how to be herself when she was already deep into functioning as part of a couple.

She tells the story of her life in order, but we all know that stories told in order contain more present than past. She is in her seventies and she is looking back. She's made it through. One day, I hope to have that narrative control, to tell a story from a happy ending. That's why, aside from natural features, Garten photographs so well. You're looking at a person who understands the self and its place in the world.

I am worried that I downplayed the problems I have listening, focusing, communicating, to everyone, but most of all to Anna, and I don't know for sure if that level of obfuscation is something my marriage can handle. I wanted her to see me as someone who could make things happen. This is why, early on, I took to the kitchen. I liked to eat and bake before her, but meeting her is what really made me a cook. I took ownership of that, made it my *whole thing*, one could say.

In one of our favorite videos of our older daughter, she wears an aqua T-shirt with a navy collar. Her ringlets are damp and glued to her forehead: it must be hot. She is at a picnic table near the lake. She has a cup of ice cream in front of her. She opens her mouth big. She has a narrow palate and a collection of large teeth. She takes a bite off a long plastic spoon. She says, *It's my favorite . . . chocolate . . . it's my favorite flavor . . .* but I only know what she's saying because she's my kid and my brain has acclimated to all the substitutions and distortions that have been at the center of our children's speech patterns. *Chocolate is your favorite flavor?* one of our sons says. His speech is also distorted, though less so. Our daughter nods. Were we trying to change them or were we trying to help them be themselves?

The physical therapist who came into our home once per week at seven in the morning, before I left for work, with her bag of puzzles, she'd put each piece on a different step, so our son would have to practice ascending and descending. *I don't want to do the stairs*, he told her once. *If you do, you'll get your sticker!* she said. *What if I don't want a sticker?* he asked. What do you say to that? Our son is a teenager and still, there is a time every few years when we will text her a picture of something we never could have imagined as she nudged him across our living room on one of those plastic floor scooters from gym class. Our son swims laps, skips three, four monkey bars with his impossibly long arms. When he jumped for the first time, in a hospital physical therapy gym where his weekly sessions involved climbing staircases to nowhere and walking on a toddler-size treadmill, Anna cried. He would have been the same person if he never walked, never ran, but I want to think we did the right thing helping along so he could. Our daughter loves to sing in the choir, has a lot to say about Dungeons & Dragons, about *The Legend of Zelda*, about *Gravity Falls*. She has a lot to say, and she can.

When the evaluators speak with me, I try to make eye contact and not to shift in my seat too many times. The current that begins in my feet and runs up my legs and back, the current telling me I must stand, I try to quiet it as much as I can. I fold my restless hands in my lap. I try to nod at the right times, but not too much. I want to smile but not at the wrong times, laugh when they pause thinking I might. Don't interrupt, my brain tells itself. In these moments, I want to appear to be the most basic white man who has ever lived. It's expected that parents function well. Otherwise, how can we be expected to consent to any of this?

But it's been there, I realize more with every year I parent, the inability to sit when it is time to sit, to stand only when it is time to stand. I am trying to focus on my children but I am seeing a whirlwind of memories of my childhood. I am four, I am eight, I am twelve and sixteen and I am not normal. I miss things people say to me, important things, because my body is telling me to stand up and go, or to blurt something out at the wrong time.

In the reports, Anna and I are some straight couple describing the ways in which our expectations of what parenting would be like have been challenged by the fact that our children are people, flawed like anyone else, with their own struggles and needs. Every report involving my own children makes my head spin.

When I drop the baby off at day care, I wear a uniform of dark denim pants or khakis with a light denim shirt. Once a few months have passed, I'm back where I started: no one would ever guess I'd given birth, not once but twice. She is a quiet baby. She prefers to be by herself. She doesn't latch well, doesn't eat well. You hold her and she just kinda looks around. When it's time to talk, she needs extra time and support to get there. She's, to no one's surprise, like all the others. By now, Anna and I just tell the doctors and therapists that this is a road we've come to know well. If these were the moments that were the central moments, then I'd say parenting isn't fun at all. But they're not the central moments. On a typical day, none of this registers.

Like Jeffrey Garten, the baby's favorite food is roast chicken. She eats it off the bone, slides pieces of it off a plate into her mouth, dips it in this or that sauce, eats it atop rice or stuffed in a quesadilla. I want her to have fun, I want to have fun. People talk about postpartum depression like it's something you only feel early on, but really, it can last a while, and it changes like anything else. In her first weeks, it felt sharp and hard, and I used Ina Garten as my escape. I watched her in her garden, watched her snip tarragon and rosemary, I felt her hydrangeas could save me. She entertained, set beautiful tables, made cheese boards. I couldn't see the beauty in everyday life, in the toys and the bottles and the dinners. I thought about Ina Garten sending brownies to Jeffrey when they were first dating, I thought about me making Anna brownies when we were first dating. Getting better isn't linear, because nothing can change who you are at the core.

I resolve to contact a neuropsychologist the day I hit another car with mine coming out of the CVS parking lot on Cumberland and Aramingo. There is always a mix of cars pulling in and out at blazing speed, and cars parked for too long, sometimes overnight, while the occupants sleep. Back in my car after running the errand, I was thinking about whatever it is I think about when I'm supposed to be focusing, about my job my writing my marriage my family, and I didn't see the young woman who was right in front of me, in her little black car.

I stepped out, expecting to be screamed at. It's Philadelphia, after all. But when the woman saw whatever was on my face—the naked horror at losing my attention so abruptly, the relief that no one had been hurt—she softened. *It's okay*, she said. *My car is fine.* She touched the bumper softly, and I knew then she loved the car. *Mine too*, I said. I'd barely looked. *I'm just really sorry, again.*

The neuropsychologist has a young, gentle face. We are meeting nearly two years after the car accident. It has taken that long to follow through. He nods when I tell him that I feel I am best suited to things like laundry and tidying. Seeing past today overwhelms me. He doesn't ask any questions about my gender or my queerness. I failed to be attentive long before I failed to be a girl. Though isn't there a problem I have, with envisioning the future, because I don't know how a person like me can exist in a future? Never mind. Those are questions for another day. The neuropsychologist is taking notes. He wants to know when my problems began. It is time for my own disability narrative. In this moment, inattention suffuses every moment of every day of every year I can remember.

From a report dated 11/16/23

Krys

experienced issues with executive functioning for as long as he could remember

pursuing an evaluation was "20 years in the making."

said he worries and ruminates daily;

feels overwhelmed by tasks that have multiple steps

intends to be an equal partner

acknowledged not following through on commitments

had intrusive thoughts about driving his car off the road

has forgotten about medical appointments, activity practices for his children, and plans with others

described zoning out during conversations, forgetting about what others have said,

has had persistent difficulties with focus, sustained attention, distractibility, forgetfulness, organization, procrastination, listening, and finishing tasks.

meets criteria for the following diagnoses

- *Attention-deficit/hyperactivity disorder, predominately inattentive presentation, moderate (F90.0)*
- *Generalized anxiety disorder (F41.1)*
- *Major depressive disorder, recurrent episode, moderate, with peripartum onset (F33.1)*

Laurie

Touch grass, the saying goes. My older children keep getting older, and they're now developing their own relationships to devices and how to use them in a way that brings meaning, knowledge, connection, without taking over everything real. How to tell them the biggest reason to touch grass is so they don't end up like me? I survived these years, but I lost myself in them too.

Because I'm their parent, it's no surprise that whatever limits Anna and I set, somebody is bound to hide a handheld Nintendo under their pillow or lock themselves in a closet with a Chromebook. *Let's take both our phones and plug them in*, I tell my oldest child, my only Gen Z kid, a freckled teenager taller than I am, a person endless miles from the baby who once lay in my useless twenty-five-year-old arms screaming, *and go touch grass together*. I ruffle his reddish hair.

With the first three, we were always joking about the most coveted toddler item: the Step2 Whisper Ride Cruiser, a toy buggy we could never convince ourselves we needed, but which each child would drift toward at any playground. And then there it was, on our local Buy Nothing group. When we plug in our phones, my son and I strap his sister into this facsimile of a vehicle and take the baby on a walk around the block, talking to her about the world and our lives, expecting nothing in return.

And okay, sometimes I have an older kid with me and we talk weather or what are you learning in school or if you could have only one Pokémon to walk every virtual world with you, which would it be, but other times I take the baby on walks on my own, and when I do, I can't say I ever leave my phone behind. I have an endless series of the same picture of my hand and my daughter. On occasion, you have to take a picture of your life to remember that it's real.

When Anna first takes all four of the children out of the house, leaving me home alone to do what I wish with my time, I wonder how I have come to live so much of my life through the food content I watch on screens. I think of all the things I have cooked that I saw first on the internet, all the things I still have left to cook or bake, all those tabs, and along with the warmth you come to feel toward anything objectively harmless that you're addicted to, I have started to feel a revulsion at the idea of opening my laptop or scrolling Instagram. I'm done with it. And anyway, the more I write about food, the stranger the algorithm becomes. As the baby has gotten older, as she has taken on a meaning beyond my own hopes and pain, something of a start to independent life, sitting, crawling, reaching for her favorite foods and turning her head toward others, my phone has stopped showing me videos of children eating and mothers cooking. Even the devices themselves are telling me I need to step away.

The next time Anna leaves the house with all the children, I read Laurie Colwin. In *More Home Cooking*, her second book of essays about cooking simply and exuberantly for friends and family, Colwin writes, *There is nothing that puts a crimp in your cooking style like the arrival of a baby. It is hard to whip the egg whites wholeheartedly when at any moment your infant may wake up from her nap and require you.*

Somehow, among the colossal onslaught of social media posts and viral essays I've seen, about mom rage, the mental load, housework-as-labor, abolishing the family, nothing has made me feel as seen as these two simple sentences. Because Colwin is able to say it's hard, but her writing is also full of joy-in-cooking, and in relating that to her parenting.

At the end of this essay, called "A Harried Cook's Guide to Some Fast Food," Colwin shares a recipe, as she does at the end of each of the short essays in *More Home Cooking*, as she did in its predecessor, *Home Cooking*. This time, it's Katharine Hepburn's Brownies, a short recipe that takes up less than half a page.

Make these brownies with a roast chicken and some veggies, Colwin advises, and *everyone will think you are wonderful for having made this monumental effort on their behalf.*

I want everyone to think I am wonderful. Is that so much to ask? It's coming up on a year since I had our last baby. If I thought the pandemic broke my functioning, that shift was nothing compared to what this child has done to me. She was a desperately wanted baby, a baby I was told I likely could not have, and I try to look at her and see her simply as she is, with her squishy fat feet like little proofed dinner rolls, her swollen pink gums exploding with new teeth. She likes food best when she eats it directly out of my hands. Into the bowl of chana masala my fingers go. They grasp a chickpea, which I smush between my forefinger and thumb before holding it out toward her lips. I want to focus on these things, these moments of doing exactly what I'm supposed to, but instead, I find myself looking at her and thinking about how she broke me. I want to be reliable, I tell my neuropsychologist, and I know I am not. The thing is, if you saw me, you would see someone constantly in motion. The only things that I do reliably are things are in front of me every day: laundry and food and washing counters and floors, shooing people to bed and dragging them out again a few hours later. I buy coffee, I fill the lined cone with scoops of grounds, I pull out the canister and hold it under the faucet. I flip the switch. I walk from room to room collecting empty mason jars, the remnants of so many glasses of water. Anna comes home after a shift and I pick up her work bag and put it on a hook, I pick up her shoes and put them on a rack, I serve her a plate of food. I hardly ever sit.

That's the thing I keep coming back to: I have struggled so much, and yet I have put dinner on the table every single night. In the worst times, I have made what Colwin might call *nursery food. Dishes such as shepherd's pie and chicken soup are a kind of therapy*, she writes.

She goes on. *I have managed to stretch the term nursery food like Silly Putty, and under its pliant heading comes a wide variety of dishes: fried chicken, lamb stew, macaroni and cheese, meatballs, baked beans, lentil soup, chili, baked stuffed potatoes, and lasagna.* The kinds of things, Colwin writes, that a guest would never call the worst thing: *interesting*.

She is describing the kitchen that is mine, and also that of most of the other harried parents I know. Come to my house and you'd see a picture of decent functioning, every child with a cubby holding a backpack, a jacket, a place to put their shoes. A drawer with some pencils and a sharpener. Every child with an assigned seat at the table, half-decent table manners. A protein a starch a vegetable, usually a dessert. A bathtime, a bedtime. Wipe the counters for the morning, start the dishwasher.

But zoom out and see the wreckage of the big picture.

As much as I want to, I cannot manage to book a babysitter, sign a child up for camp, or remember when a monthly math club meets. I don't know any of the passwords or when any bill comes due. When I open up our family's digital calendar, I struggle to find the date I was wondering about, and right away I am distracted by a buzz or a beep from another app or by someone asking me for something before I recall why I opened the calendar. I feel I deserve an award for putting the parent-teacher conference into the calendar the moment I reserve the spot, only to learn later I dropped the event on the wrong day.

If I was born in another time, would I be fine? Laurie Colwin died young, in 1992, and so she didn't have to live and parent in the timeline I'm living through. In an era of paper and talking to people in person, of needing to do the thing in front of you and not also the distant, digital thing, maybe it would have felt reasonable. If I didn't have children, would I be fine? Why waste time thinking about living my life on a plane I can't touch?

The way my thinking gets away from me. I often need to begin thoughts again in order to complete them. A circling back, a constant return to the beginning. *Are you remembering*, Anna starts, before saying something I have certainly never heard in my life. Have I? Why should I remember *that the kids have a half day Wednesday / that I switched shifts next week / that you said you'd walk the neighbor home from school / that you said you'd handle the pediatrician appointments tomorrow?* I really said these things? When? Yes, I'm told, they've been on the calendar for weeks now, and we've discussed them, sometimes more than once. The amount of energy I spend trying not to forget things I'll probably forget is astounding. I want one spot where I always put my keys. I want to buy a kid a new pair of shoes before the old ones are, one day, suddenly too raggedy to wear to school one more time. I want to book a flight months in advance. I want to set goals. I want to accomplish something that isn't right in front of me. My new daughter's birth certificate has my name spelled incorrectly but the thought of sending the form to change it nearly destroys me. *Mother's Name: Kyrs Belc.* There are so many steps to doing it, and it's made even more complicated by the multiple name changes I've had. At this point in my life, the only reason I haven't had top surgery is that I don't have my shit together enough. One day, I want my tits the fuck gone, and then I remember how hard it is for me to follow through on way more basic shit. I want to find my other daughter a guitar teacher but how do you even do that? Two of our children need braces, to start an endless series of appointments at the local orthodontist. Open enrollment is coming, but I haven't read past the first page of the new insurance packet. It's so many pages and I can barely make it to the end of a movie, let alone this pdf with its charts and network maps. I don't want to, can't, sit down and look at that.

I don't tend to stay seated long, not even when I'm reading. So I am standing in my living room reading Laurie Colwin, who tells me that if I make these brownies, people will think I'm wonderful, and I want that. That is what, I'm ready to admit, I have always wanted, to slide pots of carnitas, bowls of carrot soup, layered birthday cakes, in front of my flaws, a screen to cover over the chaos I feel inside me.

Colwin is right. Brownies do impress. They've always been the dessert I make when I really piss Anna off, or when I've said I'd bake for some event and have mismanaged my time, and now I can't wait for a cake to cool before frosting, can't proof a dough. Start to finish, you can have a warm pan of brownies out of the oven thirty minutes after the thought occurs to you, if you practice as much as I have.

The brownie recipe in *More Home Cooking*, Katharine Hepburn's, isn't anything special, but it does have less flour than most, a quarter cup to the half cup that my recipe calls for. Like the brownies that have become my front-of-mind, memorized, one-bowl go-to, these were meant to comfort cleanly and simply. When Hepburn died, a woman named Heather Henderson wrote in to *The New York Times* to describe how she came to have this recipe. As a young woman, Henderson told her father she was planning to drop out of Bryn Mawr College. She doesn't really explain why, just says she wasn't doing well, and thought she'd go abroad to write plays. (Who hasn't had this feeling of wanting to drop out of your life for a while?) Henderson's father, who did not know Katharine Hepburn but who frequently saw her grocery shopping in his neighborhood, wrote to her, asking her as a neighbor and a Bryn Mawr alum to intervene on Henderson's behalf. Hepburn called Henderson on the phone early one morning and began yelling at her about her foolishness. *What a damn stupid thing to do!* Henderson recalls her saying. And then Hepburn had Henderson, whom she'd browbeaten into remaining in college, over for tea and brownies, along with her father.

It'd make sense if the story ended there, but it doesn't. Henderson's father goes on to visit Hepburn a few more times, including when she's recovering from an accident. He brings brownies, which she tastes before declaring, *Too much flour!* If part of writing nonfiction is knowing when to stop, in my estimation, Henderson has gone on a beat too far.

There's also the issue of the recipe itself. Colwin's reproduction in *More Home Cooking*, which she says she got thirdhand—a friend encountered it in a magazine article about Hepburn—uses two ounces of unsweetened chocolate, versus the half cup of cocoa called for in the letter to the editor and in the reproduction in the *Times* cooking app, where the recipe has garnered a 5-star rating and over twelve thousand votes. Over a thousand people have taken time out of their day to review Hepburn's recipe.

The allure of a writer like Laurie Colwin, to me, is the forcefulness of her voice, of her opinions. Of course, like any decent home baker, I know that there are voices I trust, tastes I trust, and those are worth more than twelve thousand strangers' ideas. Every woman I write about has built her expertise in a different way, and Colwin has done it mostly through the writing itself, through telling her readers about the self she becomes in the kitchen.

No one who cooks cooks alone, Colwin writes, of the way a cook like us carries their influences with them every time they step through the threshold into their kitchen.

In the NYT Cooking video "The Secret to Katharine Hepburn's Brownie Recipe," Vaughn Vreeland wears a confounding outfit: white tank undershirt beneath a tight, short-sleeve button-down, sleeves rolled, inexplicably buttoned only at the bottom button, tucked into navy trousers, without a belt. I watch the place the button touches his waistband as he stirs, measures, pours. Why is this heinous outfit so sexy to me? He spends 11:30 making this simple recipe, which seems absurd, except for the fact that I like to watch him. Like so many guys like me, I like men more after transition. I like his beard and his voice and the way he reads contributor's comments aloud in a comical way that is more like joking with them than laughing at them. Sometimes he takes a load of viewer comments on a popular recipe and tests out the modifications regular people make, without sneering at the comments section the way so many do. I think that if Laurie Colwin were still alive, she would like him, his combination of sassy takes and flexibility.

Wait, are you watching a video with a man in it? Anna asks as she walks by my desk.

And here, a diversion. Why, I must ask myself, is nearly everyone I care about in food a woman? On YouTube, I scroll through *The New York Times* food creators: there's Melissa Clark, there's Claire Saffitz, there are Alison Roman videos from before they let her go. But there are others too: Priya Krishna, Sohla El-Waylly, Samantha Seneviratne. And I make their recipes. I check their cookbooks out from the library and follow the recipes carefully, propping the big, beautiful books just so, away from the splatter. I learn. But it's a simpler relationship; I don't scrutinize their outfits, I don't think about how they construct the selves they share with their audiences, I don't dream myself into their real or imagined kitchens. And I hardly ever watch the men, which has been true for forever. With rare exceptions, they bore me.

By all accounts, being a man in the kitchen may be the only thing I've figured out how to have a little success at. I'm beginning to think the white women I watch represent, each in her own way, the kind of gendered failure that is my earliest source of shame. I could have been Sara Moulton, could have had varsity-athlete-turned-varsity-mom energy, could have been Ree Drummond, making vats of macaroni and sheet cakes for my dirty, cowboy-booted kids, could have been a white woman in the kitchen, cooking for my family in a way that made perfect sense to even the most boring person I could meet.

As a child, I studied women too. They were the parents of the children I taught at a local tae kwon do studio. I studied their nails and their handbags and the way their jeans fit. The working moms, the stay-at-home moms, the divorced moms.

The dowdy moms and the hot moms. I tried to learn the culture of women, or at least the white women I had access to, growing up where I did, when I did. More than the moms who sat in the waiting room as I taught their children to kick and punch, I loved the women who took the adult tae kwon do classes with me, loved the ceremonious way they slipped rings off their fingers and unclasped their necklaces, the way they smiled at me warmly enough that there were times I thought a few of them wouldn't be embarrassed to have someone like me as a daughter. The confusing minutes of sparring with these women, who hit me with a kind of tenderness—it was then I knew I loved women, more than men by a long shot, and I felt hot shame all over. These women were the same age as my own mother, who never sat and watched us, who rolled up in her Suburban and shooed us out on the curb, because there were so many of us and she had so many places to go, because that was her sacrifice, the caring.

I remember how I idolized the women who taught at the school with me, their strength and their ponytails and the tough way they spoke to the teenage boys, who were on the verge of being too old to listen to a woman in this confusing landscape of leisure and combat, even one wearing a black belt. I would stand in the back of the room when they taught and listen to the roar of local children yelling *Yes ma'am!* when given a command. These women made me feel that life was possible. But I failed to grow up to be like them or to be any of the women my parents offered me as options. They saw what I was, but they didn't have the words to nail it quite right. Instead, they said things about my future, things like *West Point*, things like *gym teacher*. Or, they said, I could be a lawyer arguing in a courtroom, in a pantsuit, like on TV. They knew I acted hardened to the world for some reason they could not quite put a finger on, and I hid from them all my young life what was soft underneath.

The thing is, there's a parallel universe in which I became Alison Roman, stayed hard, made fun of every man in every room I ever entered, learned how to apply harsh lipstick. Growing up, there were other girls who couldn't stay still, others kind of like me, but unlike the ones with bad grades and poor classroom manners, I liked books. I could sit just enough to get by, to fly under the radar. The only person I ever hit for real, not sparring at the tae kwon do school, I mean hit them like I meant it, was the only girl tougher, more masculine, than I was. It was at recess and I took a closed fist right to her hardened stomach with all my might. She had called my brother a retard, and though I didn't have the real word for what he was, for what so many in my family are, I knew this was reason enough to really take it to the only person in my world failing worse at being a girl.

On an episode of the podcast *Sentimental Garbage*, novelist Caroline O'Donoghue, who isn't much of a cook, gets a lesson on Laurie Colwin from her friend Ella Risbridger, author of multiple books on food and cooking. Risbridger, who calls *Home Cooking* a *cult food book*, claims that just as Brian Eno said everyone who bought a Velvet Underground album went on to start a band, everyone who reads Colwin goes on to write a cookbook.

Of Colwin's chatty recipes, O'Donoghue says, *They don't feel like they existed in a hermetically sealed bubble away from the world. They just feel like part of the landscape of this, like, life that you love being in with her, and you love just being with her while she cooks.*

Perhaps most of all, it seems Risbridger is enamored of Colwin's relationship to failure. Risbridger literally wrote a food book called *Midnight Chicken* and yet, soon before recording the episode, made a crappy chicken dinner for some friends. Is there a way Colwin might reframe this as no big deal? After all, years after her death, her husband remembered that Colwin *was a great cook but the disasters were kind of fabulous*, including a red snapper that looked *like Hieronymus Bosch's vision of hell.* I love the idea of appealing to a woman who's been dead for thirty years because your dinner was mediocre. Someone who writes wisely about everyday life is bound to have a forgiving core.

She's just never gonna make you feel bad about yourself, Laurie Colwin, says Risbridger. *Even though she does very noble things like bakes her own bread and volunteers at shelters, I never feel like she's a better person than I am.*

In an essay to mark what would have been Colwin's eightieth birthday, Mia Manzulli reflects on rereading Colwin's books, which she first encountered as a graduate student in the early '90s. Like Rachel Syme, who called Colwin the *bard of burgeoning adulthood*, Manzulli found much meaning in exploring Colwin as someone who really knew how to write about women figuring it all out. Reading her decades later, though, Colwin takes on a new meaning: *What I see now and never appreciated at 25 is the underlying messiness; that has become Colwin's ultimate gift to me. I have the Wedgwood china, but the dinners are not always elegant or inventive; the house is lovely, but the dining room table serves double duty as my desk; the friendships are old and deep, and too often long-distance.*

Manzulli reflects on a phrase from Colwin's own writing, used in her fiction: *domestic sensualist.* She quotes Colwin's childhood friend, the writer Willard Spiegelman: *Laurie the writer and the person was a "strong domestic sensualist," whose interest in home, kitchen, and domesticity was a means of keeping disorder at bay and of controlling one's surroundings. The drive for perfection or precision compensates for the equally strong counter-tendency to sloppiness and emotional upheaval.*

When your baby is born at home, the decision to take them outside for the first time is just that, a decision. Otherwise, I will keep draping my soft, vulnerable body around her sleeping body in bed, crying, on loop. I make my way downstairs and lay a pillow on the concrete stoop just so. We are stoop sitters, Anna and me, we like to sit with coffee or a beer or ice pops and watch the people in our neighborhood, though, I must admit, this more often than not leads to us seeing someone who is up to no good.

On that same stoop, I introduce my daughter to the world. I hold her still-wrinkled body out with both hands. I've always had an easy time handling babies. I support my daughter's head with my opened right hand, the other hand under her diaper. It all feels ceremonial. Her entire back fits along my forearm. I am her place. *There's a whole world out there*, I tell her, though I am not Mufasa and she's not Simba, we're on a dirty corner of Kensington watching wispy pieces of trash get swept up by the wind, and off in the distance, if she could see beyond a few inches in front of her face, she might catch a teenager on a bike roaming around looking for packages to steal. But it's our block, our world. The light of today's sun is the brightest thing my daughter has ever seen. She squints and wiggles and grunts in her first moments as part of the real world.

The story becomes realer, more controlled, to me, as I tell it again and again. It takes on a sort of actualization, an embodiment. Not in the way I explained it to my therapist, who only saw the rawness of it, she was all, *trauma this, trauma that*, doing right by me and my nervous system but also making me shrug off her grave concern in a flippant sort of way. It's when friends start to come over again that I find the words: *home birth, retained placenta, no epidural, because, you know, no hospital!* They look to my face to decide how to react and I see that, and I'm grateful for it. Sometimes I want laughs, and other times the sad, sympathetic looks work. It's around the big table in my living room, our everything table, our breakfast lunch dinner homework everybody's desk table, that I feel most comfortable asserting control over my own story. I serve friends brunch, which feels like the easiest meal to handle. I don't have to get up early or start making it in the dim afternoon hours when my patience and attention begin to wane. Over eggs in purgatory and cinnamon rolls, baby draped over my shoulder, and then sitting on my lap, and then sitting in a high chair, as she ages her way through these meals, I compose a narrative of pain and, in it, begin to find a narrative of recovery.

The idea of a dinner party is rather like the idea of a novel, Laurie Colwin writes. *Just as novels are not necessarily written from beginning to middle to end (although they end up that way), it is easier to think about a dinner party course by course, but not consecutively.*

Somehow or other I always end up in a kitchen feeding a crowd. This essay, called "Feeding the Multitudes," represents a small ripple in the persona Colwin has cultivated. In earlier essays, she's confident, authoritative, weaving her personal spicy takes on food and cooking (*How depressing it is to open a cookbook whose first chapter is devoted to equipment. / Take beef stew, that favorite of brownie and girl scout leaders for cooking projects. People are always messing it up, mostly men. / There is no such thing as really bad potato salad*) with tried-and-true recipes from her own kitchen. But in "Feeding the Multitudes," she admits perhaps the real reason she's taken to cooking: *For the socially timid, the kitchen is the place to be*. It's a way for her to socialize, to help out when Students for a Democratic Society strike when she's at Columbia, and a way for her to volunteer. The insular Colwin of earlier essays, who's trying to get her daughter to eat a vegetable and to calm those who are afraid of getting their own dinner on the table, comes through so clearly here: cooking is a predictable way to participate, a way to craft a persona inflected with confidence.

In the era of going viral, a content creator's child can be many things. She can be part of the content itself, to cute or moving or troubling or even evil effect. You can show your daughter learning to walk, enjoying life's small pleasures, picking a dandelion or trying out a playground swing. Or you can show her having a tantrum. If she's disabled, you can caption the video, *Early signs my daughter was autistic*, for example, or *Reasons we homeschool my intellectually disabled daughter*. Delivery room, pediatrician visit, prom date, the choice is yours what and when to expose. Or she can be off-screen: *Meals I prep every Sunday* or *How I organize my daughter's toys*, but you never see the daughter. We all have to make our own choices. Laurie Colwin died before the big shift to digital, missed blogging, the eGullet Forums, Epicurious, Allrecipes, the NYT Cooking app, YouTube, Instagram. Colwin's death came just a few years after marketing experts started tossing around words like *brandscape* to describe the proliferation of life-as-market, market-as-life, brand or be ground into nothingness.

There were parents in her fiction, and she was a parent in her nonfiction. Her one child, who was elementary school aged when she died, figures prominently in her food writing. In *Home Cooking*'s "Fish," Colwin talks about her transformation into a *fish lover*, after growing up with little exposure to adventurous fish eating: *As I watch my daughter taste her first this and that—which, in New York City, means her first shiitake mushroom, falafel, plate of hummus, tree ear, bamboo shoot or chocolate mousse—I remember back to that time when my palate was clear and unsophisticated, everything was an adventure and the world was as fresh as a fish.*

This idea of the blank-slate-ness of childhood, of her child's childhood, is complicated by Colwin's essay "My Daughter, My Self," published in *Allure* just over a year before her death. Colwin, whose child came to understand their nonbinary gender fully only after years of trialing life as a boy, was known to their mother only as *a daughter who came howling into life, shrieking like a tormented chicken*, a delightfully odd child who was *fixated on cats* and who pleasured in the discovery that *her hair was a kind of fiber art and could be arranged in any number of ways*—hairstyles she goes on to request, from Colwin, as if picking off a menu.

Colwin writes about her sometimes tortured quest to raise a child free from the idea that a woman's looks are paramount. *Sometimes at night I lie in bed trying to clarify what I want for her*, Colwin writes. Colwin is happy that her child can wear jeans to school and play on soccer teams and have mothers who, like Colwin, are career women.

When her child asks Colwin if they will be pretty as a teenager, Colwin is seized with love and fear. *I want her to be able to walk past a mirror without consulting it and to be free to concentrate on millions of things more important than how she looks.*

I don't want to smooth out Colwin, to make her just a feel-good feminist mom. She was judgy as hell, too, someone you'd want to share the bench with at the park and dish about which parents you judged the hardest. Born in November, my daughter is old enough to sit on the ground propped up by my legs while I gossip this way from the ground with my own neighbors. In a 1990 interview with Mickey Pearlman, Colwin says she is *surrounded by people who work and are in a constant snit about what to feed their kids . . . What happens is that these Yuppie parents go out and eat all these extraordinary things . . . and their kids are eating these really disgusting things.*

She connects this wayward set of parenting moves, feeding kids peanut butter and hot dogs instead of the foods their parents eat, with the way parents' hysteria about gender seeps into their parenting and thus restricts their children: *You can do a lot to dispel these things but then you look around and everywhere you go, little boys have short hair and are very 'butch' and little girls have ruffles. It's parents, it's the culture, and it takes a lot to make sure you don't end up with one of those nasty stereotypic children.*

Colwin's child's response came, decades later, in an essay, also published in *Allure*: *If little girls could truly be anything, it would not be unthinkable if one turned out to be a boy—would it?*

I wish that she could see how I am becoming, however bumpily and painfully, exactly what she wanted me to be: myself.

When children are very young and you are in the world of toilet training and applesauce pouches and day care payments, there is a sense in which you are holding on for a promised future of companionship and understanding. I am now again in the world of a baby, but I am in the other world too: my sons are my height and they want to discuss novels, world events, the social hierarchy of the seventh grade. They can make grilled cheeses and fry eggs, and one day, I sleep through my Saturday get-up-before-the-baby alarm and come downstairs to find my daughters sitting at the table together, one feeding the other yogurt from a plastic cup. *Dada's awake!* the older one yells, and applauds like a little girl, but in the performative way you do when you're not in that stage of life anymore.

Colwin's fiction has a reputation for happy endings, something that apparently did not please her. In an interview with Dennis Zhou in *The New Yorker*, her child says that *Laurie didn't like the simple answer, and the simple answer is that her books all have happy endings . . . That scene marked the end of the story, sure, but it's easy to see all the interconnected lives of her characters continuing beyond what she'd written.*

The narrator of Colwin's "Evensong," a story published in 2023 after spending many years in a box in a storage unit, is a woman having an affair. The unnamed narrator is a list maker—*I am by nature a person whose constant battle against encroaching chaos is fought by list-making and organizational thinking.*

When the narrator begins having an affair with a family friend, food noise becomes a harbinger of this encroaching chaos. *I spent many hours of each day thinking as follows: If Louis turns up for lunch and eats the boiled potatoes, we will have to have rice with parsley and butter with dinner, but if he does not eat the potatoes we can have potato salad, which goes so much better with roast chicken.*

One day, after they have sex, her lover drags her to an Evensong service at a nearby seminary, though she protests that she isn't even a Christian! She finds herself moved to tears by the music and by the *shock that Louis knew this service like the back of his hand and seemed on very chummy terms with his Creator.*

The end of the story is happy, in its way. Lives are changed but not ruined, and the narrator gets to continue going to the chapel, though she does not convert. *It's nice in there*, she tells her husband. *I like to sing. It reminds me of my Jewish heritage.* As readers, we are privy to a level of complexity that her husband and child aren't: the place is about Louis as much as it's about singing, or God.

Colwin told Mickey Pearlman in 1990 that she feels *strongly Jewish* despite her *assimilated* childhood. Colwin is someone with *many feelings about God with no particular vessel to put them in*, which pains her, since she believes that human beings *have longings which can only be called religious, and they have to be answered in some way.*

I am in my midthirties and finding Colwin at just the right time. I wasn't ready when I was twenty, when I was twenty-five, when I was thirty. While Colwin's characters and most other people were cooking in shoebox-size apartments and figuring it all out, I was having one kid after another, because they were desperately wanted, and also, I must admit now, because I was desperately masking.

After a lifetime of rejecting the Catholic upbringing that taught me I was wrong, I find myself lingering outside the Quaker meetinghouse by our home. It's a simple building and I think most of the people who stand at a nearby intersection holding homemade posters begging for ceasefires across the globe worship there. I haven't gone in, and maybe I won't, but I might, and recognizing the pull is the key right now. And perhaps more than that, I know I can sit with myself for an hour or two. *My friends and I realized that most of us are neurodivergent*, one of my kids tells me as we walk to the subway together. He kicks a rock and another rock and I wonder what would have happened to me if I'd thought about this twenty-five years ago. *Well, doesn't that make sense?* I ask. You come from the family you come from, I come from the family I come from. *Take one capsule by mouth one time daily.* A stimulant medication isn't going to make me feel like my life is meaningful and needs to go on, but being able to listen to my child, to tune in and stay there, is a start. No wonder I found the best version of myself I could find, standing over a countertop, moving my every limb. What will I be able, or rather what will I *get*, to do now?

Colwin writes in *More Home Cooking*, *A person cooking is a person giving: Even the simplest food is a gift*. I am thinking about the day of the embryo transfer, of the sharp pain of a nurse pressing down on me while my doctor, whose kindness was crystal clear just from the wrinkles around her eyes, put my daughter inside me. I was told to take it easy for the rest of the day, and I had follow-up questions about this, namely what kinds of sex I was and was not allowed to have in the week that followed, but I had forgotten to ask if I could do light housework, could make dinner. Anna offered, but I wanted to feel like it was a regular day, so I said I would make something that I could mostly sit and do. I remember sitting on the stool by the stovetop stirring macaroni and cheese, the sharp cheddar, the mustard powder, the tray of roasted broccoli, the way everything tasted better when you knew your luck was maybe about to turn.

Is there anything better than the pleasure of eating the exact sweet you want when you want it? I know my life has not been upturned completely because I still lose myself in dessert, in making it and in eating it. I make Ina Garten's lemon yogurt loaf and drink in the rich lemony scent wafting through the house, lovingly pour lemon syrup over the hot cake to soak it, glaze the cake with more sugar and lemon when it's cool. I make Claire Saffitz's pistachio buns, giving my stand mixer a workout late at night making the milk bread–inspired enriched dough, waking in the morning to a cold, domed, fluffy vehicle for nuts and cardamom and demerara sugar. I roll out a giant rectangle, spread honey butter over it, sprinkle pistachios and spices and lemon zest over, roll, slice, proof, and bake. The first bun is heaven, and the second is too much, but I eat it anyway, watching around the table as my children tear into the spirals. I make that Alison Roman buttermilk cake, because it's a weeknight and I have buttermilk that's been sitting in the fridge for too long, and we eat it standing around the counter, pulling the thick glaze off our forks with the force of our whole mouths. *This is so good*, someone says.

I'm able to enjoy it, too, don't remain stuck in what the cake was for me, how some days before and after I had the baby, it really felt like the only good thing. It can be something else now. My baby is almost one and I'm not better, but I'm starting to think I will be. Like Laurie Colwin, I make my own birthday cakes. The first one after the baby is Julia Moskin's Funfetti-inspired cake. I pour in the sprinkles, push the bright-white frosting around the sides with an offset spatula.

More sprinkles and then I eat a big slice before taking my new Rollerblades on a spin around the block. That birthday may be when things start to turn. In the months that follow, I walk my neighborhood pushing a stroller, or I bike across town, delivering cupcakes, cookies, croissants, kouign-amann wrapped in tinfoil. Maybe I am wonderful. On my next birthday, I make Claire Saffitz's three-layered carrot cake with brown butter cream cheese frosting, putting my aging, ailing stand mixer to one of its last tests. And I love doing it, love making the exact thing I want and sharing it. But I don't always need to do it alone.

One night, it's a struggle to get dinner on the table. Anna is between night shifts, so she's sleeping while I have to prepare the meal, and then she'll be out the door soon after it's over. Dinner, homework, bathtime, bedtime, it's all on me tonight. I am cleaning while I am cooking, trying to save myself work. The baby is in a carrier and then she's in her seat in the kitchen and then she's back in the carrier. I'm sweating. The rice cooker sings. The chicken sets off the smoke detector. At the table, we pass the baby back and forth while we eat, because she doesn't want to stay in her seat. The other kids want to help, but getting from desire to actualization requires so much coaching on my part, and I don't have the energy. The table is still smeared with hummus and chicken grease and half the dishes are in the sink when one of the kids asks to go to the ice cream truck. I want to say no, but I don't. *Okay*, I say, *let me find some cash.*

Outside, the kids stand on the stoop, silent, stock-still, listening for Mister Softee's song. I lug the stroller down the steps and we head out, walking in a pack up one block and then the next, stopping at each corner to lean in and listen. We falsely hear it. Each time we have had a baby, Anna and I have noted that, in the shower, we hear a baby's cry, even when it's not there. It's one of the things that makes those months so hard, feeling like you don't have time or space to do even the most basic self-care. No matter how asleep the baby is when you put them down, no matter how fast you jump in the shower and begin scrubbing, you hear it, a faint, echoey wailing, a reminder that you're not alone, that your time isn't yours. If you're not needed now, you're on the verge of being needed. But never mind that—the baby is old enough now to be plopped on the ground with a sibling and a box of toys while I shower, and she's old enough for a few licks of an ice cream cone if we can ever find the truck. There isn't ever a phase with young kids that lasts forever, not with my kids, and finally, now, the phases of this last one's life are turning over at a clip. It's hot, August in Philadelphia, the sun still blazing even though it's nearly bedtime, and people are outside, sitting on stoops, biking in the middle of the street. We walk and walk. My kids are giving one another flat tires, stepping on the backs of the Crocs in front of them, and shoving one another as we approach each corner.

And then, just as I'm about to say we should take our cash and get packaged ice cream bars from a corner store freezer, we hear it. Our heads turn. One by one, my children tear down the street toward the sound and the truck, its side emblazoned with three magical words: *SUNDAES. SHAKES. CONES.* The kids are vibrating with pleasure before the words even come out of our mouths. We all want the same thing, who wouldn't? One rainbow sprinkle cone and another and another, and then, finally, one more for me. Three dollars to change your day, maybe even your life. It's about to be the most beautiful thing.

Acknowledgments

Thank you to Stella Parks, Sara Moulton, Bridget Lancaster, Julia Collin Davison, Claire Saffitz, Deb Perelman, Alison Roman, Ree Drummond, and Ina Garten. I don't know any of you, but I'm grateful to you all the same. The small parts of your talents and selves you have shared aren't just a springboard I used to jump off into my own creative waters; they've also been a life raft for me through some of the most difficult years of my life. Thank you for all you have shared with the world. To the late Laurie Colwin, thank you for writing two food books I have carried back and forth between home and the office more times than I can count. And thank you to RF Jurjevics for providing me with a copy of Laurie's essay from *Allure*. It was an honor to engage with both of your writing.

The primary parties responsible for this book's existence are the day care providers, teachers, noontime aids, school administrators, bus drivers, and after-school-program workers who worked with my four children during its writing. I believe in and celebrate public education. Thank you to the physical therapists, occupational therapists, speech and language pathologists, social workers, and school psychologists who met my family where we were and who truly celebrate disabled people's inclusion in our society and world. Everyone, disabled and nondisabled, needs and will benefit from the inclusive world you are helping to make. I am in debt to the City of Saint Paul's commitment to fun and wonderful free after-school programming and athletic leagues at its recreation centers. I am grateful my family is among the relatively small percentage of American families today who can afford high-quality day care while we await the blessed day our last child begins public education. If you have cared for my children, you have cared for me.

I appreciate my coworkers at the public schools where I learned to be a teacher, which is a very specific way of learning who you are and who you want to be. Thank you to all my students, to whom I hope I gave a small part of my best self.

It's awe-inspiring to see the work that happens at the oncology clinic where I worked after finishing graduate school in creative writing. I especially thank the four brilliant neuropsychologists whose insights into our patients structured much of my day-to-day labor, and the rest of the psychosocial team for modeling rigorous care. Thank you, Hannah, Megan, Iris, and Kelly.

In the years I worked in that clinic, which comprised the first three years I worked on this book, I struggled to find time and space to be creative. I appreciate Jennifer Wilson, Hannah Howard, and Terese Marie Mailhot, who led community workshops where I read and wrote and felt like it still mattered. Thank you to my peers in those classes, especially those in Terese's workshop at Tin House.

Thanks to my colleagues and students at the University of Minnesota, where I've been lucky enough to work as a fellow in the creative writing program as I figured out what I was really trying to say in this book, and why. Thanks especially to Megan Giddings and Pete Mason.

Sara Ryan, thanks for writing and gossiping with me on Zoom for all these years, and for telling me to "put more memoir in your memoir." Thanks to all the members of the online writing group Tiswit, proud to put another book on our collective shelf. Thank you to Kate Dean for long neighborhood walks when I was struggling the most, and to Maggie Wachter for being my parenting lifeline. Thank you to Jess Nambudiri for talking food and parenting and books with me at work and after.

Thanks to the editors at *Electric Literature*, *beestung*, and *The Kenyon Review* who published earlier drafts of parts of this book.

My agent, Ashley Lopez, is the only person who saw a bit of all the structures I tried on to tell the story of my food-content obsession, and I appreciate her sticking with the project and with me. Thanks to everyone at Catapult, many of you for the second time. Thank you, Alicia Kroell.

There are not thanks enough for Dr. Jackie Gutmann, whose steady, no-nonsense compassion for me as a fertility patient still causes my chest to soar a little when I remember those months on my way to her clinic. Mac VanTillburg, thank you for delivering Anna safely in my cozy, crowded bedroom and for handling the minor emergency after like a damn boss! Thank you, Payj Thommes and Kim Martino and Rachel Utain-Evans, for being there with us. Steph Brown and Cara Puff, you are very good lactation consultants! Shout-out to Dr. Nicole Ludwig Fernandez for compassionate pelvic floor therapy—something that should be standard of care for postpartum people. Thank you, Lesha Vozobule, Joe Ling, Hannah Wydeven, Garrett Ferderber, Cate Reynolds, and the other coaches at Novem Community Fitness and Solcana Fitness for keeping me moving. Obviously, I need it.

Seanie, Sammy, Z, and AJ, you are very cool kids. Let's never get too old for Mario Party or for the playground, okay?

Anna Belc, I am sorry I do so many things that warrant apology brownies. Thank you for helping to orchestrate my highest highs and for staying through my lowest lows.

Thank you to Riverwards Produce for stocking the most beautiful strawberries. Thank you to Islam for driving the world's best Mister Softee truck right by my own Philadelphia home.

Thank you to everyone who has ever sat down at my dinner table. I hope you come back soon.

References

Stella

Kolbe, Winrich, dir. "Darmok." *Star Trek: The Next Generation*. Season 5, episode 2. Written by Joe Menosky. Featuring Patrick Stewart and Paul Winfield. Aired September 30, 1991. Paramount.

Parks, Stella. *BraveTart: Iconic American Desserts*. W. W. Norton & Company, 2017.

Parks, Stella. "Homemade Cheez-Its." YouTube, uploaded by Serious Eats, September 30, 2016. www.youtube.com/watch?v=1a6nvR9lXlk.

Parks, Stella. "How to Make Texas Sheet Cake." YouTube, uploaded by Serious Eats, May 8, 2018. www.youtube.com/watch?v=R4eVZH36UHg.

Parks, Stella. "How to Make the Best Blueberry Pie." YouTube, uploaded by Serious Eats, July 17, 2018. www.youtube.com/watch?v=yLDba8jgAWQ&t=157s.

Parks, Stella. "How to Make the Best Brownies." YouTube, uploaded by Serious Eats, April 10, 2018. www.youtube.com/watch?v=x7Yz2ZuS5bo.

Parks, Stella. "That's a Job? Pastry Scientist and Best-Selling Author: Stella Parks." Interview by Amy Madore. *Juggle*, January 28, 2019. thejuggle.blog/thats-a-job/stella-parks/.

Wikipedia. "Sara Moulton." Accessed December 12, 2025, 5:58 p.m. en.wikipedia.org/wiki/Sara_Moulton.

Sara

Collins, Kathleen. *Watching What We Eat: The Evolution of Television Cooking Shows*. Bloomsbury Academic, 2009.

Higgins, Laurie. "Sara Moulton's Accidental Culinary Career." *Cape Cod Times*, May 16, 2007. www.capecodtimes.com/story/lifestyle/food/2007/05/16/sara-moulton-s-accidental-culinary/52897682007/.

Kemper, Benjamin. "Sara Moulton's Long-Overdue Autopsy of 1990s Food Culture." *Saveur*, December 1, 2022. www.saveur.com/culture/sara-moulton-interview-food-1990s/.

Moulton, Sara. "Cooking Live with Sara Moulton - Burgers." YouTube, uploaded by Allan Smithee, January 6, 2020. www.youtube.com/watch?v=IgAVpdtct1M.

Moulton, Sara. "Full Exclusive Interview with Sara Moulton." KLCS. klcs.org/full-exclusive-interview-with-sara-moulton-2/.

Moulton, Sara. *Sara Moulton Cooks at Home*. Broadway Books, 2002.

Moulton, Sara. "Vegan with Adam Sobel." YouTube, uploaded by Sara's Weeknight Meals, February 4, 2017. www.youtube.com/watch?v=bZBZqk3x_4w.

Ray, Rachael. "Rachael Ray at Home." Interview by Christopher Kimball. *Christopher Kimball's Milk Street Radio*, December 17, 2021. www.177milkstreet.com/radio/rachael-ray-at-home.
Vider, Stephen. *The Queerness of Home*. University of Chicago Press, 2021.

Bridget and Julia

America's Test Kitchen. "Beef Tacos." May 1, 2012. *America's Test Kitchen*. www.americastestkitchen.com/recipes/180-beef-tacos.
America's Test Kitchen. "Quick and Easy Cream Biscuits." *America's Test Kitchen*. September 1, 2005. www.americastestkitchen.com/recipes/576-quick-and-easy-cream-biscuits.
Christle, Heather. *The Crying Book*. Catapult, 2019.
Davison, Julia Collin. "How to Make Murgh Makhani (Indian Butter Chicken)." YouTube, uploaded by America's Test Kitchen, December 21, 2021. www.youtube.com/watch?v=ZkvbDBocgMk.
Davison, Julia Collin, and Bridget Lancaster. "How to Make Simple Stovetop Mac and Cheese." YouTube video, uploaded by America's Test Kitchen, May 26, 2019. www.youtube.com/watch?v=POnornXjoMc.
Davison, Julia Collin, and Bridget Lancaster. "How to Make the Absolute Best Ground Beef Chili." YouTube, uploaded by America's Test Kitchen, March 13, 2019. www.youtube.com/watch?v=nuuS_uBpRd4.
Davison, Julia Collin, and Bridget Lancaster. "You Need to Make These Life Changing Homemade Pecan Sticky Buns." YouTube, uploaded by America's Test Kitchen, March 13, 2018. www.youtube.com/watch?v=aZT4S-MFZao.
Fairman, Matthew. "Hot Sesame Noodles with Pork." *America's Test Kitchen*. March 27, 2019. www.americastestkitchen.com/recipes/11595-hot-sesame-noodles-with-pork.
Fielding-Singh, Priya. *How the Other Half Eats: The Untold Story of Food and Inequality in America*. Little, Brown Spark, 2021.
Goodman, Makenna. *The Shame*. Coffee House Press, 2020.
July, Miranda, dir. *Me and You and Everyone We Know*. FilmFour, 2005.
Lancaster, Bridget. "Bridget Lancaster Loves Teaching People How to Cook." Interview by Terrence Doyle. America's Test Kitchen Online, September 23, 2019. www.americastestkitchen.com/articles/432-bridget-lancaster-loves-teaching-people-how-to-cook.
Lancaster, Bridget. "Full Exclusive Interview with Bridget Lancaster." KLCS. klcs.org/full-exclusive-interview-with-bridget-lancaster-2/.
Lancaster, Bridget. "Learn to Cook: Bridget Lancaster Explains How to Chop an Onion." YouTube, uploaded by America's Test Kitchen, September 5, 2023. www.youtube.com/watch?v=Znv46pRiDIk.

Souza, Dan. "Oatmeal Muffins." *America's Test Kitchen*. September 5, 2013. www.americastestkitchen.com/recipes/7275-oatmeal-muffins.

Claire

Clark, Melissa. "Chocolate Babka." *NYT Cooking*. Updated December 29, 2025. cooking.nytimes.com/recipes/1018045-chocolate-babka.

Collins, Kathleen. *Watching What We Eat: The Evolution of Television Cooking Shows*. Bloomsbury Academic, 2009.

The Female Quotient (@femalequotient). "Even the Queen of Soul had to face the daily dilemma of what to make for dinner. We can totally relate!" [video of Aretha Franklin]. Instagram, December 16, 2023. www.instagram.com/reel/C07GJC_PI6w/?hl=en.

Johnson, Rebecca May. "I Dream of Canteens." *Dinner Document*, April 30, 2019. dinnerdocument.com/2019/04/30/i-dream-of-canteens/.

Marzano-Lesnevich, Alex. "How Do I Define My Gender if No One Is Watching Me?" *New York Times*, April 2, 2021. www.nytimes.com/2021/04/02/opinion/transgender-nonbinary-pandemic-transition-.html.

Raymond-Speden, Emma, et al. "Intellectual, Neuropsychological, and Academic Functioning in Long-Term Survivors of Leukemia." *Journal of Pediatric Psychology* 25, no. 2 (2000): 59–68. doi.org/10.1093/jpepsy/25.2.59.

Saffitz, Claire. "At 13, Claire Saffitz Was Almost Too High Strung to Enjoy Her Bat Mitzvah." Interview by Samantha Leach. *Spiel*, December 15, 2020. samanthaleach.substack.com/p/at-13-claire-saffitz-was-almost-too.

Saffitz, Claire. "Claire Makes Sourdough Crêpes Suzette." YouTube, posted by Bon Appétit, April 3, 2020. www.youtube.com/watch?v=Ze9jxpur47M.

Saffitz, Claire. "Claire Saffitz Makes Carrot and Pecan Cake." YouTube, uploaded by Claire Saffitz x Dessert Person, December 31, 2020, www.youtube.com/watch?v=ou3zjoRoGus.

Saffitz, Claire. "Claire Saffitz Makes Soft & Crispy Focaccia." YouTube, uploaded by Claire Saffitz x Dessert Person, December 3, 2020. www.youtube.com/watch?v=NGnMrM9qDtE&t=317s.

Saffitz, Claire. "Claire Saffitz Makes Walnut Maple Sticky Buns." YouTube, uploaded by Claire Saffitz x Dessert Person, March 18, 2021. www.youtube.com/watch?v=JlzmsTiOJnU.

Saffitz, Claire. "Claire Saffitz Teaches Amateur How to Make Croquembouche." YouTube, uploaded by Claire Saffitz x Dessert Person, May 6, 2021. www.youtube.com/watch?v=OwQlEF8DXs8.

Saffitz, Claire. *Dessert Person*. New York: Clarkson Potter, 2020.

Saffitz, Claire. "Pastry Chef Attempts to Make Gourmet Girl Scout Cookies." YouTube, uploaded by Bon Appétit, March 17, 2020. www.youtube.com/watch?v=m-gYY5cR8M8.
Severson, Kim. "How the Cookbooks of 2020 Tell the Stories of Our Pandemic Kitchens." *New York Times*, March 2, 2021. www.nytimes.com/2021/03/02/dining/best-cookbooks-2020-pandemic.html?searchResultPosition=4.
Talbot, Margaret. "Les Très Riches Heures de Martha Stewart." *New Republic* 214, no. 20 (1996): 30.
u/bactoria. "35% of the way through Dessert Person, another 65% to go." r/clairesaffitz, Reddit, 2023. www.reddit.com/r/clairesaffitz/comments/1avpz9b/35_of_the_way_through_dessert_person_another_65/.
u/vivahermione. Comment on "Is it wrong to hope for people not to have kids?" r/childfree, Reddit, posted by u/manganatsu101, 2020. www.reddit.com/r/childfree/comments/l1ygyg/is_it_wrong_to_hope_for_people_not_to_have_kids/.

Deb

Goldfield, Hannah. "Deb Perelman Is Thankful for Tacos." *New Yorker*, November 25, 2020. www.newyorker.com/culture/the-new-yorker-interview/deb-perelman-is-thankful-for-tacos.
Hazan, Marcella. "Marcella Hazan's Bolognese Sauce." Adapted by *New York Times*. Updated December 29, 2025. cooking.nytimes.com/recipes/1015181-marcella-hazans-bolognese-sauce.
Laperruque, Emma. "Looking Back at 10 of Our Favorite Bloggers' First Posts." *Food52*, April 27, 2018. food52.com/story/22204-looking-back-at-10-of-our-favorite-bloggers-first-posts.
Perelman, Deb. "Butterscotch Pudding Popsicles." *Smitten Kitchen*, August 28, 2013. smittenkitchen.com/2013/08/butterscotch-pudding-popsicles/.
Perelman, Deb. "Chicken and Dumplings." *Smitten Kitchen*, December 11, 2007. smittenkitchen.com/2007/12/chicken-and-dumplings/.
Perelman, Deb. "Corn Salad with Chile and Lime." *Smitten Kitchen*, July 12, 2019. smittenkitchen.com/2019/07/corn-salad-with-chile-and-lime/.
Perelman, Deb. "Deb Perelman Is Thankful for Tacos." Interview by Hannah Goldfield. *New Yorker*, November 25, 2020. www.newyorker.com/culture/the-new-yorker-interview/deb-perelman-is-thankful-for-tacos.
Perelman, Deb. "Deb Perelman: Smitten Kitchen." Interview by Ethan Frisch. *Why Food?*, March 5, 2021. heritageradionetwork.org/episode/deb-perelman-smitten-kitchen/.

Perelman, Deb. "Freedom, Ringing." *Smitten Kitchen*, June 30, 2006. smittenkitchen.com/2006/06/freedom-ringing/.
Perelman, Deb. "Hot Fudge Sundae Cake." *Smitten Kitchen*, July 18, 2013. smittenkitchen.com/2013/07/hot-fudge-sundae-cake/.
Perelman, Deb. "The 'I Want Chocolate Cake' Cake." *Smitten Kitchen*, February 26, 2015. smittenkitchen.com/2015/02/the-i-want-chocolate-cake-cake/.
Perelman, Deb. "Lasagna Bolognese." *Smitten Kitchen*, February 12, 2012. smittenkitchen.com/2012/02/lasagna-bolognese/.
Perelman, Deb. "Look What We Baked!" *Smitten Kitchen*, September 19, 2009. smittenkitchen.com/2009/09/look-what-we-baked/.
Perelman, Deb. "Quick Pasta and Chickpeas." *Smitten Kitchen*, October 5, 2017. smittenkitchen.com/2017/10/quick-pasta-and-chickpeas-pasta-e-ceci/.
Perelman, Deb. "Pumpkin Bread." *Smitten Kitchen*, October 13, 2016. smittenkitchen.com/2016/10/pumpkin-bread/.
Perelman, Deb. "Short Rib French Onion Soup." *Smitten Kitchen*, December 16, 2021. smittenkitchen.com/2021/12/short-rib-onion-soup/.
Perelman, Deb. *Smitten Kitchen Keepers*. Knopf, 2022.
Radtke, Kristen. *Seek You: A Journey Through American Loneliness*. Pantheon, 2021.
Zapata, Isabel. *In Vitro: On Longing and Transformation*. Translated by Robin Myers. Coffee House Press, 2023.

Alison

Abad-Santos, Alex. "How Alison Roman Became the Reluctant, Pasta-Loving 'Prom Queen of the Pandemic,'" *Vox*, April 22, 2020. www.vox.com/2020/4/22/21222868/alison-roman-shallot-pasta-pandemic-cooking.
Carle, Eric. *The Very Hungry Caterpillar*. World of Eric Carle, 1994.
Collins, Lauren. "Alison Roman Just Can't Help Herself." *New Yorker*, December 13, 2021. www.newyorker.com/magazine/2021/12/20/alison-roman-just-cant-help-herself.
Connors, Joanna. "How a Transplanted Face Transformed Katie Stubblefield's Life." *National Geographic*, September 2018. www.nationalgeographic.com/magazine/article/face-transplant-katie-stubblefield-story-identity-surgery-science.
Cox, John. "Thirty Years with the Edinburgh Postnatal Depression Scale: Voices from the Past and Recommendations for the Future." *British Journal of Psychiatry* 214, no. 3 (2019): 127–29. doi.org/10.1192/bjp.2018.245.

Cox, John, Jeni Holden, and Carol Henshaw. "The Edinburgh Postnatal Depression Scale." In *Perinatal Mental Health: The EPDS Manual*. Cambridge: Royal College of Psychiatrists, 2014.

DeGeneres, Ellen. *Ellen DeGeneres: For Your Approval*. Directed by Joel Gallen. Recorded at the Orpheum Theatre, Minneapolis, MN, August 17, 2024. Released September 24, 2024. Netflix, www.netflix.com/title/81037130.

DeGeneres, Ellen. "Here and Now." Recorded at Beacon Theater, New York, May 2, 2003. Aired on HBO June 25, 2003.

McKinnon, Kate. "Kate McKinnon's Tribute to Ellen DeGeneres - 2020 Golden Globes." YouTube, uploaded by NBC, January 5, 2020. www.youtube.com/watch?v=1owY3QPg4Bc.

Porter, Kevin T. (@KevinTPorter). "Right now we all need a little kindness. You know, like Ellen Degeneres always talks about! She's also notoriously one of the meanest people alive Respond to this with the most insane stories you've heard about Ellen being mean & I'll match every one w/ $2 to @LAFoodBank." Twitter, March 20, 2020, 12:12 p.m. x.com/KevinTPorter/status/1241049881688412160.

Roman, Alison. "Alison Roman's Chicken Confit | NYT Cooking." YouTube video, 12:13. Uploaded by NYT Cooking, June 4, 2019. www.youtube.com/watch?v=2DY88WeZmLY.

Roman, Alison. "Baked Ziti." *NYT Cooking*, February 18, 2025. cooking.nytimes.com/recipes/1018954-baked-ziti.

Roman, Alison. "The Best Meatball Recipe | Home Movies with Alison Roman." YouTube, uploaded by Alison Roman, January 26, 2021. www.youtube.com/watch?v=O2swHDv4XNw.

Roman, Alison. "Creamy Cauliflower Pasta with Pecorino Bread Crumbs." *NYT Cooking*, April 16, 2019. cooking.nytimes.com/recipes/1020173-creamy-cauliflower-pasta-with-pecorino-bread-crumbs.

Roman, Alison. *Dining In*. Clarkson Potter, 2017.

Roman, Alison. "Pizza Party | Home Movies with Alison Roman." YouTube, uploaded by Alison Roman, October 4, 2022. www.youtube.com/watch?v=W61WBGNYwIw.

Roman, Alison. "Slow-Roasted Citrus Salmon With Herb Salad." *New York Times*, February 10, 2020. cooking.nytimes.com/recipes/1018972-slow-roasted-citrus-salmon-with-herb-salad.

Roman, Alison. "What Alison Roman Wants." Interview by Dan Frommer. *New Consumer*, May 7, 2020. newconsumer.com/2020/05/alison-roman-interview/.

Saxena, Jaya. "What Exactly Is Going on Between Chrissy Teigen and Alison Roman on Twitter?" *Eater*, May 11, 2020. www.eater.com

/2020/5/11/21254554/chrissy-teigen-alison-roman-twitter-fallout-explained.
Zinoman, Jason. “Ellen DeGeneres Is Not as Nice as You Think.” *New York Times Magazine*, December 12, 2018. www.nytimes.com/2018/12/12/arts/television/ellen-degeneres.html.

Ree

Autostraddle. “PHOTO GALLERY: Queer in the Kitchen.” January 27, 2027. www.autostraddle.com/photo-gallery-queer-in-the-kitchen-367133__trashed/?all=1.
Batey, Eve. “The Strange but True Story of the Pioneer Woman's Link to Killers of the Flower Moon.” *Vanity Fair*, October 19, 2023. www.vanityfair.com/hollywood/2023/10/the-strange-but-true-story-of-the-pioneer-womans-link-to-killers-of-the-flower-moon.
Drummond, Ree (@thepioneerwoman). “Pantry organization/restock Part 1!” [video of Drummond restocking baking items in a large pantry]. Instagram, August 28, 2022. www.instagram.com/reel/ChoL1ONpu_3/.
Drummond, Ree. *The Pioneer Woman Cooks: Food from My Frontier*, William Morrow Cookbooks, 2012.
Fortini, Amanda. “O Pioneer Woman.” *New Yorker*, May 2, 2011.
“Home on the Ranch.” *The Pioneer Woman*. Featuring Ree Drummond. Aired August 27, 2011. Food Network.
Matthiesen, Sara. “The Discipline of Family: Queering the History of Reproductive Labor.” *GLQ: A Journal of Lesbian and Gay Studies* 30, no. 4 (2024): 541–45. doi.org/10.1215/10642684-11331042.
Murray, Ruby H. “An Osage Looks at the Pioneer Woman.” *Iowa Review* 52, no. 2 (2023): 29–41, 237.
Petersen, Sara. *Momfluenced*. Beacon Press, 2023.
Rainey, Clint. “The Pioneer Woman Is America's 23rd-Largest Landowner.” *Grub Street*, November 15, 2017.
Sittenfeld, Curtis. “The Prairie Wife.” *New Yorker*, February 5, 2017. www.newyorker.com/magazine/2017/02/13/the-prairie-wife.
Slagle, Ali. “Rosemary-Garlic Roasted Chicken and Gnocchi.” *New York Times Cooking*. Updated February 3, 2022. Accessed June 19, 2023. cooking.nytimes.com/recipes/1022960-rosemary-garlic-roasted-chicken-and-gnocchi

Ina

The phrase “too much of a muchness” is attributed to Matthew Gavin Frank.

Garten, Ina. "Baked Cod with Garlic and Herb Ritz Crumbs." In *Modern Comfort Food*. Clarkson Potter, 2020.

Garten, Ina. *The Barefoot Contessa Cookbook*, Clarkson Potter, 1999.

Garten, Ina. "Beattie's Chocolate Cake." In *Barefoot Contessa at Home*. Clarkson Potter, 2006.

Garten, Ina. *Be Ready When the Luck Happens*. Crown, 2024.

Garten, Ina. *Cooking for Jeffrey*, Clarkson Potter, 2016.

Garten, Ina. "Ina Garten: At Home with the Barefoot Contessa." Interview by Katie Couric. *Next Question with Katie Couric*, April 20, 2017.

Garten, Ina. "Ina Garten: Cooking Is Hard." Interview by David Remnick. *New Yorker Radio Hour*, December 16, 2022.

Garten, Ina. "Ina Garten's Parmesan Smashed Potatoes." Interview by Al Roker. *Cooking Up a Storm with Al Roker*, November 1, 2021.

Garten, Ina (@inagarten). "It's Always Cocktail Hour in a Crisis!" [video of Ina Garten making a cosmopolitan cocktail]. Instagram, April 1, 2020. www.instagram.com/reel/B-cJUwUpxbM/.

Garten, Ina. "Julia Gets Wise with Ina Garten." Interview by Julia Louis-Dreyfus. *Wiser Than Me*, April 17, 2024. omny.fm/shows/wiser-than-me/julia-gets-wise-with-ina-garten.

"Halloween for Grownups." *Barefoot Contessa*. Season 9, episode 10. Featuring Ina Garten. Aired October 20, 2007. Food Network.

Heti, Sheila, and Sarah Manguso. "Episode 37: Sheila Heti and Sarah Manguso." Interview by Rachel Zucker. *Commonplace*, September 19, 2017. commonplace.today/commonplace-podcast/episode-37-sheila-heti-and-sarah-manguso.

MacRoy-Higgins, Michelle, and Carlyn Kolker. *Time to Talk: What You Need to Know about Your Child's Speech and Language Development*. AMACOM, a division of American Management Association, 2017.

Manguso, Sarah. "The Grand Shattering." *Harper's Magazine*, August 2018. harpers.org/archive/2015/08/the-grand-shattering/.

Moskin, Julia. "How Does Ina Do It?" *New York Times*, November 16, 2020. www.nytimes.com/2020/11/16/dining/ina-garten-barefoot-contessa.html.

Laurie

Colwin, Laurie. "Evensong." *New Yorker*, April 17, 2023.

Colwin, Laurie. *Home Cooking: A Writer in the Kitchen*. Vintage, 1988.

Colwin, Laurie. *More Home Cooking: A Writer Returns to the Kitchen*. Vintage, 1993.

Colwin, Laurie. "My Daughter, My Self." *Allure*, June 1991.

Garten, Ina. "Lemon Yogurt Cake." *Barefoot Contessa*. 2006. barefootcontessa.com/recipes/lemon-yogurt-cake.

Henderson, Heather. "Straight Talk from Miss Hepburn; Plus the Actress's Own Brownie Recipe." *New York Times*, July 6, 2003. www.nytimes.com/2003/07/06/nyregion/l-straight-talk-from-miss-hepburn-plus-the-actress-s-own-brownie-recipe-400831.html.

Jurjevics, RF. "My Mother, Myself: To My Mom, Who Wrote for *Allure* About Parenting Me in 1991." *Allure*, March 25, 2019. www.allure.com/story/my-mother-myself-laurie-colwin-rf-jurjevics.

Manzulli, Mia. "In Praise of the Domestic Sensualist: Laurie Colwin at 80." *Literary Hub*, June 14, 2024. lithub.com/in-praise-of-the-domestic-sensualist-laurie-colwin-at-80/.

Nelson, Candice. "Rainbow Sprinkle Cake." Adapted by Julia Moskin. *New York Times*. cooking.nytimes.com/recipes/1018364-rainbow-sprinkle-cake.recipes/1018364-rainbow-sprinkle-cake.

O'Donoghue, Caroline. "Home Cooking by Laurie Colwin." *Sentimental Garbage*, August 5, 2020. podcasts.apple.com/us/podcast/home-cooking-by-laurie-colwin/id1444729607?i=1000487261505.

Pearlman, Mickey, and Katherine U. Henderson. *Inter/View: Talks with America's Writing Women.* Lexington: University Press of Kentucky, 2015.

Risbridger, Ella. *Midnight Chicken: & Other Recipes Worth Living For.* London: Bloomsbury, 2019.

Saffitz, Claire. "Pistachio Morning Buns." *New York Times*. Updated February 29, 2024. cooking.nytimes.com/recipes/1022249-pistachio-morning-buns.

Syme, Rachel. "Laurie Colwin's Recipe for Being Yourself in the Kitchen." *New Yorker*, October 11, 2021. www.newyorker.com/magazine/2021/10/18/laurie-colwins-recipe-for-being-yourself-in-the-kitchen.

Vreeland, Vaughn. "The Secret to Katharine Hepburn's Brownie Recipe | NYT Cooking." YouTube. Uploaded by NYT Cooking, July 1, 2022. www.youtube.com/watch?v=vBySJoleYwM.

Zhou, Dennis. "Laurie Colwin's Child on Finding 'Evensong.'" *New Yorker*, April 10, 2023.

© K Ho

Krys Malcolm Belc is the author of *The Natural Mother of the Child: A Memoir of Nonbinary Parenthood* and the flash nonfiction chapbook *In Transit*. His recent essays have been featured in *The Kenyon Review*, *Electric Literature*, *The Arkansas International*, and elsewhere. Belc is the memoir editor of *Split Lip Magazine*. He lives in Saint Paul, Minnesota.